# Quick QUILTS for

HOME

## BY DEBBIE MUMM

Create warm and welcoming rooms featuring handmade quilts and accessories using the 50 projects and ideas in this book as inspiration. From table quilts to throws, wallhangings to pillows, chair covers to bed quilts, you'll find beautiful home décor projects for every place in your home.

©2010 by Debbie Mumm • Leisure Arts, Inc., 5701 Ranch Drive, Little Rock, AR 72223 • www.leisurearts.com

# Table of Contents

## Dear Friends,

Don't you feel that quilters are particularly blessed! You've got the best hobby in the world plus the talents to update your home with custom created throws, wallhangings, pillows, and table toppers. With so many fabrics to choose from it is easy to coordinate colors to fit any room.

This book is about sewing for the home. Jazz up your living room with new pillows and a throw, add warmth to the kitchen with table runners and chair covers, relax in a room with spa-friendly accessories, enjoy summertime living in colorful outdoor comfort, and inspire your creative place with storage, baskets, and wallhangings.

Enjoy the creative process, and then enjoy the end results – every day, in every way, in every room.

Love,
Debbie Mumm

## Living SPACES

## Gathering PLACES

# Outdoor RETREATS

# Relaxation ROOMS

# Creative CORNERS

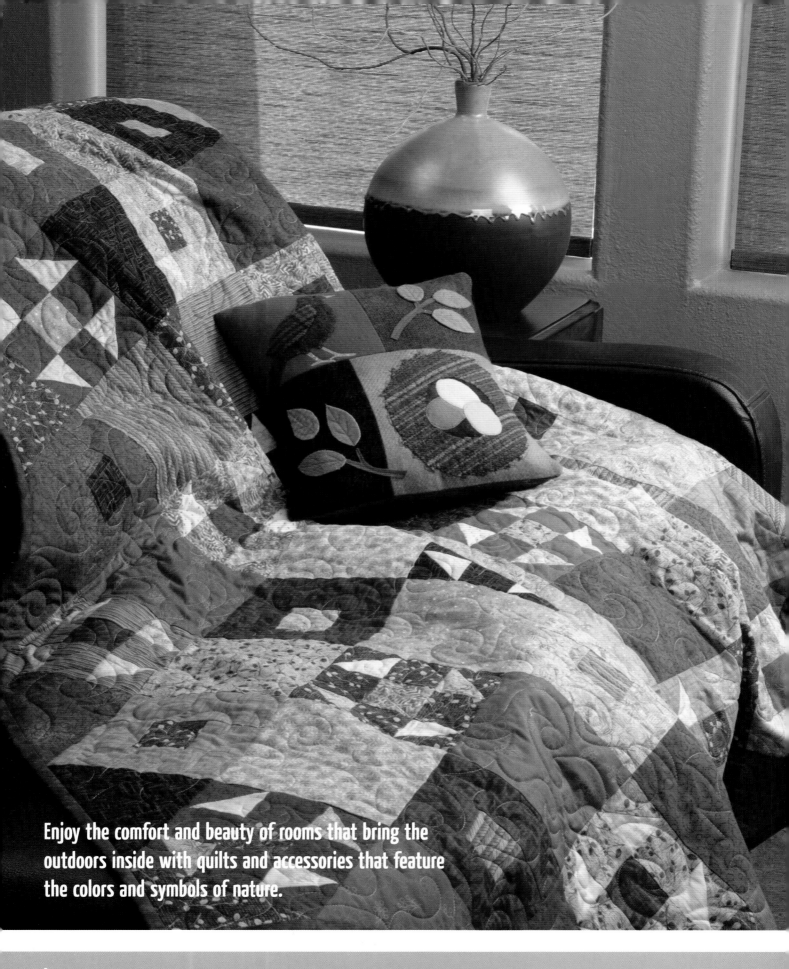

Enjoy the comfort and beauty of rooms that bring the outdoors inside with quilts and accessories that feature the colors and symbols of nature.

# Living SPACES

# Natural Living LAP QUILT

| Natural Living Lap Quilt Finished Size: 52" x 69" | FIRST CUT | | SECOND CUT | |
|---|---|---|---|---|
| | Number of Strips or Pieces | Dimensions | Number of Pieces | Dimensions |
| **Fabric A** Darks ½ yard each of 7 Fabrics  | 1* | 9¾" x 42" | 1* | 9¾" square** **cut twice diagonally |
| | | | 3* | 6½" squares |
| | | | 4* | 6½" x 2½" |
| | 1* | 3" x 42" | 4* | 3" squares |
| | 1* | 2½" x 42" *cut for each fabric | 16* | 2½" squares |
| **Fabric B** Mediums ½ yard each of 7 Fabrics 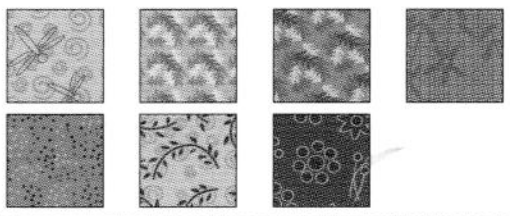 | 1* | 6½" x 42" | 3* | 6½" squares |
| | | | 4* | 6½" x 2½" |
| | 1* | 3" x 42" | 4* | 3" squares |
| | 1* | 2½" x 42" *cut for each fabric | 16* | 2½" squares |
| **Fabric C** Lights ⅙ yard each of 7 Fabrics 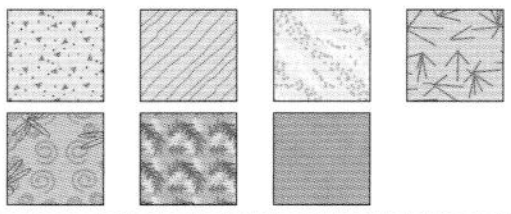 | 1* | 3" x 42" *cut for each fabric | 8* | 3" squares |
| **Fabric D** Corner Squares Assorted Fabric A Scraps each of 4 Fabrics 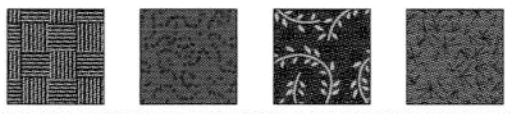 | 1* | 5⅛" squares*** *cut for each fabric ***cut once diagonally | | |
|  **Binding** ⅝ yard | 7 | 2¾" x 42" | | |
| Backing - 3⅓ yards Batting - 58" x 75" | | | | |

## Fabric Requirements and Cutting Instructions

Read all instructions before beginning and use ¼"-wide seam allowances throughout. Read Cutting Strips and Pieces on page 108 prior to cutting fabric.

## Getting Started

Light fabric accents are scattered throughout our medium/dark quilt. Blocks measure 6½" square (unfinished). Refer to Accurate Seam Allowance on page 108. Whenever possible use Assembly Line Method on page 108. Press seams in direction of arrows.

## Making Block 1

1. Sew one 2½" Fabric A square between two matching 2½" Fabric B squares as shown. Press.

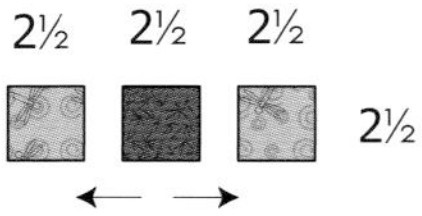

2½   2½   2½

2½

←   →

2. Sew unit from step 1 between two matching 6½" x 2½" Fabric B pieces as shown. Press. Block 1 measures 6½" square.

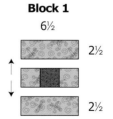

**Block 1**

6½

2½

2½

Make 24
(in assorted fabric combinations)
Block measures 6½" square

3. Using assorted Fabric A and B pieces, repeat steps 1 and 2 to make a total of twenty-four blocks varying A and B placement.

An earthy color palette and simple scrappy design give this quilt an unaffected feeling of comfort and warmth. Basic squares team with blocks sparked by center squares and triangles of soft colors to create a naturally enticing quilt.

## Natural Living LAP QUILT
Finished Size: 52" x 69"

## Making Block 2

1. Draw a diagonal line on wrong side of one 3" Fabric C square. Place marked square and one 3" Fabric A square right sides together. Sew scant ¼" away from drawn line on both sides to make half-square triangles as shown. Cut on drawn line and press. Square to 2½". This will make two half-square triangle units. Repeat step using one *different* 3" Fabric C square with one identical 3" Fabric A square.

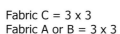

Fabric C = 3 x 3
Fabric A or B = 3 x 3

Square to 2½
Make 2
Half-square Triangles

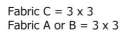

Fabric C = 3 x 3
Fabric A or B = 3 x 3

Square to 2½
Make 2
Half-square Triangles

2. Sew one matching 2½" Fabric A square between two units from step 1, one of each combination, as shown. Press. Make two identical units.

2½

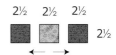

2½

Make 2

3. Sew one 2½" Fabric B square between two matching 2½" Fabric A squares as shown. Press.

2½    2½    2½

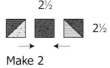

2½

4. Sew unit from step 3 between two units from step 2 as shown. Press. Block 2 measures 6½" square.

**Block 2**

Block measures 6½" square

5. Using assorted Fabric A, B, and C pieces, repeat steps 1-4 to make a total of twenty-four blocks varying A and B placement.

**Block 2**

Make 24
(in assorted fabric combinations)
Block measures 6½" square

## Assembling the Quilt

It is recommended to lay out the entire quilt prior to sewing rows together. Extra 6" Fabric A and B squares and Fabric A and D triangles were cut to give placement fabric options when laying out the quilt. Refer to photo on page 7 and layout on page 8 to arrange blocks and Fabric A and B squares and triangles.

1. Sew one Fabric D triangle to one Block 1. Press. Sew this unit between two Fabric A triangles as shown. Press. Make two and label Rows 1 and 13.

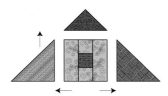

Make 2
Label Rows 1 & 13

2. Arrange and sew together two Fabric A triangles, two of Block 2, and one 6½" Fabric A or B square as shown. Press. Make two and label Rows 2 and 12.

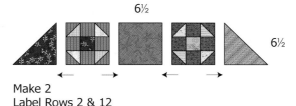

6½

6½

Make 2
Label Rows 2 & 12

3. Arrange and sew together two Fabric A triangles, three of Block 1, and two 6½" Fabric A or B squares as shown. Press. Make two and label Rows 3 and 11.

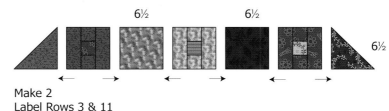

6½    6½    6½

Make 2
Label Rows 3 & 11

# It's in the details

### Nesting Instinct!

Ceramics, artwork, and found objects can reflect your natural nesting instinct. A framed print of quail eggs teams with a faux nest and a ceramic vase etched with bird silhouettes for a beautiful tabletop display. Or, group a vase and a mossy bird with a real found nest encased in a glass cloche engraved with the word "Nest."

4. Arrange and sew together two Fabric A triangles, four of Block 2, and three 6½" Fabric A or B squares as shown. Press. Make two and label Rows 4 and 10.

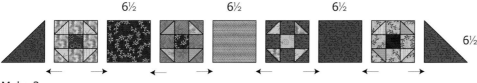

Make 2
Label Rows 4 & 10

5. Arrange and sew together two Fabric A triangles, five of Block 1, and four 6½" Fabric A or B squares as shown. Press. Make two and label Rows 5 and 9.

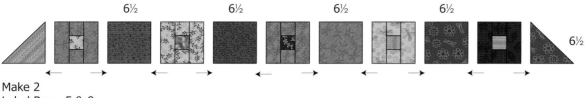

Make 2
Label Rows 5 & 9

6. Arrange and sew together one Fabric A triangle, six of Block 2, five 6½" Fabric A or B squares, and one Fabric D triangle as shown. Press. Make two and label Rows 6 and 8.

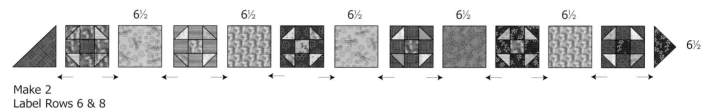

Make 2
Label Rows 6 & 8

7. Arrange and sew together two Fabric A triangles, six of Block 1, and five 6½" Fabric A or B squares as shown. Press. Make one and label Row 7.

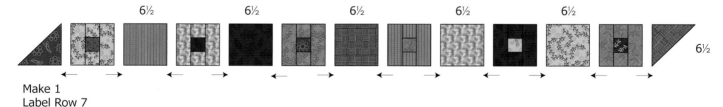

Make 1
Label Row 7

8. Referring to photo on page 7 and layout on page 8, arrange and sew together rows from steps 1-7. Press.

## Layering and Finishing

1. Cut backing crosswise into two equal pieces. Sew pieces together lengthwise to make one 60" x 80" (approximate) backing piece. Press.

2. Referring to Layering the Quilt on page 110, arrange and baste backing, batting, and top together. Hand or machine quilt as desired.

3. Refer to Binding the Quilt on page 110. Sew 2¾" x 42" binding strips end-to-end to make one continuous 2¾"-wide binding strip. Bind quilt to finish.

# It's in the details

### Nature as Decorator

Nature is a master at outdoor decorating so bringing the colors, aromas, and textures of nature indoors makes it easy to create beautiful and restful living spaces.

Rich browns, mossy greens, sky blues, and golden hues like the earthy palettes of these vases will infuse your home with the warm comfortable colors from nature. Natural elements such as twigs, grasses, sea shells, rocks, and moss bring glorious textures and organic shapes into your home.

### Mixing Metal and Moss

Mixing materials such as metal, fabric, glass, and moss creates an interesting and eye-catching display on a table or shelf. In this photo, the table quilt provides a unifying color palette for an arrangement of decorative items.

Mixing fabrics such as a nubby knitted throw on a sleek leather sofa (page 15) or mixing wool with cotton in a wall hanging (page 17) creates a delightful blend of texture and touch.

# Sweet Home WALL ART

| Sweet Home Wall Art Finished Size: 5½" x 22½" | FIRST CUT | |
|---|---|---|
| | Number of Strips or Pieces | Dimensions |
| **Fabric A** Background Assorted Scraps each of 4 Fabrics | 1* | 4½" square *cut for each fabric |
| **Fabric B** Accent Borders Assorted Scraps | 12**  8** | 1" x 5½"  1" x 4½"  **total needed cut from eight fabrics |
| **Binding** ¼ yard | 2 | 2¼" x 42"  ¼" finished binding |
| **Appliqué Letters** - Assorted Scraps  Backing - ¼ yard  Batting - 9" x 26"  Lightweight Fusible Web - ⅛ yard  Frame (optional) - 9½" x 27" or as desired | | |

## Fabric Requirements and Cutting Instructions

Read all instructions before beginning and use ¼"-wide seam allowances throughout. Read Cutting Strips and Pieces on page 108 prior to cutting fabric.

## Getting Started

Accent your wall with this scrappy art piece featuring the word "HOME". If you would like to feature a different word make additional blocks as needed and adjust frame size. Block measures 5½" square (unfinished). Refer to Accurate Seam Allowance on page 108. Whenever possible use Assembly Line Method on page 108. Press seams in direction of arrows.

## Making the Wall Art

1. Sew one 4½" Fabric A square between two different 1" x 4½" Fabric B pieces as shown. Press. Make four in assorted fabric combinations.

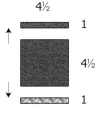

Make 4
(in assorted fabric combinations)

2. Sew unit from step 1 between two different 1" x 5½" Fabric B pieces as shown. Press. Make four in assorted fabric combinations. Block measures 5½" square.

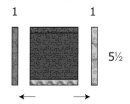

Make 4
(in assorted fabric combinations)
Block measures 5½" square

3. Arrange and sew together four 1" x 5½" different Fabric B pieces and units from step 2 as shown. Press.

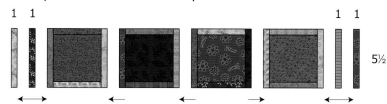

There's no place like HOME! Earthy colors complement the block letters in this simple, yet expressive, wall piece. We chose to frame this small quilt for added impact.

## Adding the Appliqués

Refer to appliqué instructions on page 109. Our instructions are for Quick-Fuse Appliqué, but if you prefer hand appliqué and add ¼"-wide seam allowances.

1. Use patterns on page 14 to trace "HOME" on paper side of fusible web. Use appropriate fabrics to prepare all appliqués for fusing.

2. Refer to photo to position and fuse appliqués to quilt. Finish appliqué edges with machine satin stitch or other decorative stitching as desired.

## Layering and Finishing

1. Referring to Layering the Quilt on page 110, arrange and baste backing, batting, and top together. Hand or machine quilt as desired. Note: We hand quilted our piece.

2. Refer to Binding the Quilt on page 110. Use 2¼"-wide Binding strips to bind quilt. Note: Finished width of binding is ¼" instead of our normal ½".

3. Select a frame larger than quilt. Center quilt on backing. Secure quilt to backing with hidden stitches. Insert into frame and hang as desired.

**Sweet Home Wall Art and Pillow**

"E" Pattern is reversed for use
with Quick-Fuse Applique (page 109).

Tracing Line  ───────────

# Sweet Home PILLOW

A quick rearrange and HOME becomes a pillow.
Make this pillow in your accent colors.

## Materials Needed

Fabric A (Background) - Scrap
(each of 4 fabrics)
> One 4½" square

Fabric B (Accent Borders) - Scraps
(cut from assorted fabrics)
> Eight 1" x 5½"
> Eight 1" x 4½"

Outside Border & Backing - ½ yard
> Two 10" x 14½"
> Two 2½" x 14½"
> Two 2½" x 10½"

Appliqué Letters - Assorted scraps

Batting and Lining - 18" x 18" each

Lightweight Fusible Web - ⅛ yard

14" Pillow Form
> OR Optional Pillow Form - ½ yard
> > Two 14½" Fabric Squares
> > Polyester Fiberfill

## Fabric Requirements and Cutting Instructions

Read all instructions before beginning and use ¼"-wide seam allowances throughout. Read Cutting Strips and Pieces on page 108 prior to cutting fabric.

### Making Blocks

1. Refer to Making the Wall Art steps 1 and 2 on page 12, to make four blocks in assorted fabrics.

2. Refer to photo to arrange and sew together two rows with two blocks each. Press. Sew rows together. Press.

3. Sew unit from step 2 between two 2½" x 10½" Outside Border strips. Press seams toward border. Sew this unit between two 2½" x 14½" Outside Border strips. Press.

### Adding the Appliqués

Refer to appliqué instructions on page 109. Our instructions are for Quick-Fuse Appliqué, but if you prefer hand appliqué add ¼"-wide seam allowances.

1. Use patterns on page 14 to trace "HOME" on paper side of fusible web. Use appropriate fabrics to prepare all appliqués for fusing.

2. Refer to photo to position and fuse appliqués to quilt. Finish appliqué edges with machine satin stitch or other decorative stitching as desired.

### Finishing the Pillow

1. Refer to Finishing Pillows on page 111, step 1, to prepare pillow top for quilting. Quilt as desired.

2. Use two 10" x 14½" backing pieces and refer to Finishing Pillows, page 111, steps 2-4, to sew backing.

3. Insert 14" pillow form or refer to Pillow Forms page 24 to make a pillow form if desired.

## Sweet Home PILLOW
Finished Size: 14" x 14"

# Nesting Instinct 2-PIECE QUILT

## Fabric Requirements and Cutting Instructions

Read all instructions before beginning and use ¼"-wide seam allowances throughout. Read Cutting Strips and Pieces on page 108 prior to cutting fabric.

### Getting Started

A great idea takes two quilts of different sizes, layers them together to get a stunning finished quilt that has both piecing and appliqué. The layers are secured together with buttons. The larger quilt blocks measure 7½" square (unfinished). Refer to Accurate Seam Allowance on page 108. Whenever possible use Assembly Line Method on page 108. Press seams in direction of arrows.

### Making the Small Appliqué Quilt

We used wool for Fabrics B, C, D, and E. These pieces need to be backed with interfacing to help prevent stretching and give body to fabric. Refer to appliqué instructions on page 109. Our instructions are for Quick-Fuse Appliqué, but if you prefer hand appliqué, reverse patterns and add ¼"-wide seam allowances to cotton fabrics.

1.  Referring to Layering the Quilt on page 110, arrange and baste backing, batting, and 18" Fabric A square together. Hand or machine quilt as desired.

2.  Refer to Binding the Quilt on page 110. Use 3½"-wide Binding strips to bind top. Note: Finished width of binding is ¾" instead of our normal ½".

3.  Following manufacturers' instructions either sew or fuse interfacing to each Fabric B, C, D, and E pieces.

4.  Sew one 6½" x 5½" Fabric B piece to one 6½" x 5½" Fabric C piece as shown. Press.

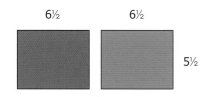

| Nesting Instinct 2-Piece Quilt Finished Size: 32" x 32" | FIRST CUT | | SECOND CUT | |
|---|---|---|---|---|
| | Number of Strips or Pieces | Dimensions | Number of Pieces | Dimensions |
| **Small Appliqué Quilt - 19" x 19"** | | | | |
| **Fabric A** Small Quilt Background ⅝ yard | 1 | 18" x 42" | 1 | 18" square |
| **Fabric B** Appliqué Background Scrap | 1 | 6½" x 5½" | | |
| **Fabric C** Appliqué Background Scrap | 1 | 6½" x 5½" | | |
| **Fabric D** Appliqué Background Scrap | 1 | 5" x 7½" | | |
| **Fabric E** Appliqué Background Scrap | 1 | 8" x 7½" | | |
| **Binding** ¼ yard | 2* | 3½" x 42" *¾" finished binding | | |
| Backing - ⅔ yard — Batting - 24" x 24" — Appliqués - Assorted wool scraps — 1" Buttons - 4 — Lightweight Fusible Web - ⅓ yard — Embroidery Floss (optional) — Interfacing (Fusible or Sew-in) - ½ yard | | | | |
| **Large Pieced Quilt - 32" x 32"** | | | | |
| **Fabric F** Block Center ⅛ yard each of 2 Fabrics | 1* | 1½" x 42" *cut for each fabric | 8* | 1½" squares |
| **Fabric G** Block 1st Accent ¼ yard each of 2 Fabrics | 3* | 1½" x 42" *cut for each fabric | 16* 16* | 1½" x 3½" 1½" squares |
| **Fabric H** Block 2nd Accent ¼ yard each of 2 Fabrics | 4* | 1½" x 42" *cut for each fabric | 16* 16* | 1½" x 5½" 1½" x 3½" |
| **Fabric I** Block 3rd Accent ⅓ yard each of 2 Fabrics | 6* | 1½" x 42" *cut for each fabric | 16* 16* | 1½" x 7½" 1½" x 5½" |
| **First Border** ⅙ yard | 4 | 1" x 42" | 2 2 | 1" x 29½" 1" x 28½" |
| **Outside Border** ¼ yard | 4 | 1½" x 42" | 2 2 | 1½" x 31½" 1½" x 29½" |
| **Binding** ⅜ yard | 4 | 2¾" x 42" | | |
| Backing - 1 yard — Batting - 36" x 36" | | | | |

6½     6½

5½

Layer these two quilts together for a stunning dimensional quilt that features both piecing and appliqué; or make one or the other and use each wherever you want color, texture, and symbols from nature.

5. Sew one 5" x 7½" Fabric D piece to one 8" x 7½" Fabric E piece as shown. Press. Sew units from step 4 and this step together as shown. Press.

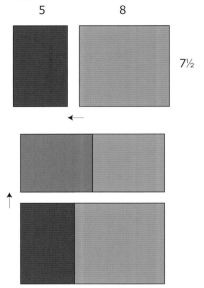

6. Use patterns on pages 20 and 21 to trace bird, nest, leaves, and stems on paper side of fusible web. Use appropriate fabrics to prepare all appliqués for fusing.

7. Refer to photo on page 17 and layout to position and fuse appliqués to unit from step 5. Finish appliqué edges with machine satin stitch or other decorative stitching as desired.

8. Refer to photo on page 17 and layout to center appliqué unit from step 7 on smaller quilt from step 2. Using a hand or machine blanket stitch, attach appliqué unit to smaller quilt's background.

Nesting Instinct Small Appliqué Quilt Layout
19" x 19"

## Nesting Instinct 2-PIECE QUILT
Finished Size: 32" x 32"

## Making the Large Pieced Quilt

1. Sew one 1½" Fabric F square between two matching 1½" Fabric G squares as shown. Press. Make sixteen, eight of each combination.

2. Sew one unit from step 1 between two matching 1½" x 3½" Fabric G pieces as shown. Press. Make sixteen, eight of each combination.

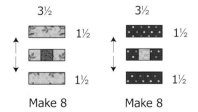

3. Sew one unit from step 2 between two matching 1½" x 3½" Fabric H pieces as shown. Press. Make sixteen, eight of each combination.

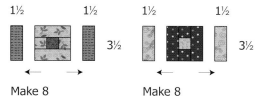

Make 8          Make 8

4. Sew one unit from step 3 between two matching 1½" x 5½" Fabric H pieces as shown. Press. Make sixteen, eight of each combination.

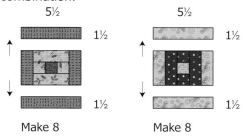

Make 8          Make 8

5. Sew one unit from step 4 between two matching 1½" x 5½" Fabric I pieces as shown. Press. Make sixteen, eight of each combination.

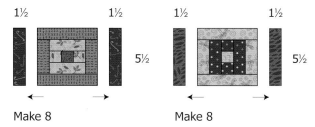

Make 8          Make 8

6. Sew one unit from step 5 between two matching 1½" x 7½" Fabric I pieces as shown. Press. Make sixteen, eight of each combination. Label one set of blocks Block 1 and the other set Block 2.

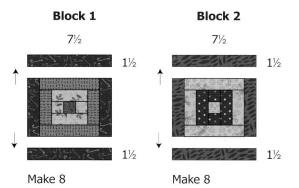

**Block 1**          **Block 2**

7½          7½

Make 8          Make 8

7. Arrange and sew together two each of Blocks 1 and 2 alternating blocks as shown. Press. Make four.

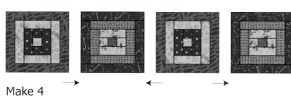

Make 4

8. Referring to photo on page 17 and layout on page 21, arrange and sew rows from step 7 together checking orientation of blocks prior to sewing. Press.

9. Sew quilt top from step 8 between two 1" x 28½" First Border strips. Press seams toward borders. Sew this unit between two 1" x 29½" First Border strips. Press.

10. Sew quilt top from step 9 between two 1½" x 29½" Outside Border strips. Press seams toward borders. Sew this unit between 1½" x 31½" Outside Border strips. Press.

11. Referring to Layering the Quilt on page 110, arrange and baste backing, batting, and top together. Hand or machine quilt as desired.

12. Refer to Binding the Quilt on page 110. Use 2¾"-wide Binding strips to bind quilt.

## Finishing the Quilt

1. Refer to photo on page 17 and combination layout on page 18 to arrange the smaller quilt on the pieced quilt.

2. Sew four 1" buttons to smaller quilt corners stitching through all layers to hold quilt in place.

**Nesting Instinct 2-Piece Quilt**

Pattern is reversed for use
with Quick-Fuse Applique (page 109).

Tracing Line _____
Tracing Line - - - - - - - - - - - - - - - -
(will be hidden behind other fabrics)

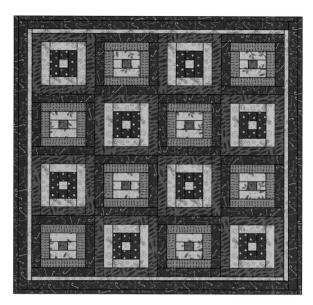

Nesting Instinct Large Pieced Quilt Layout
32" x 32"

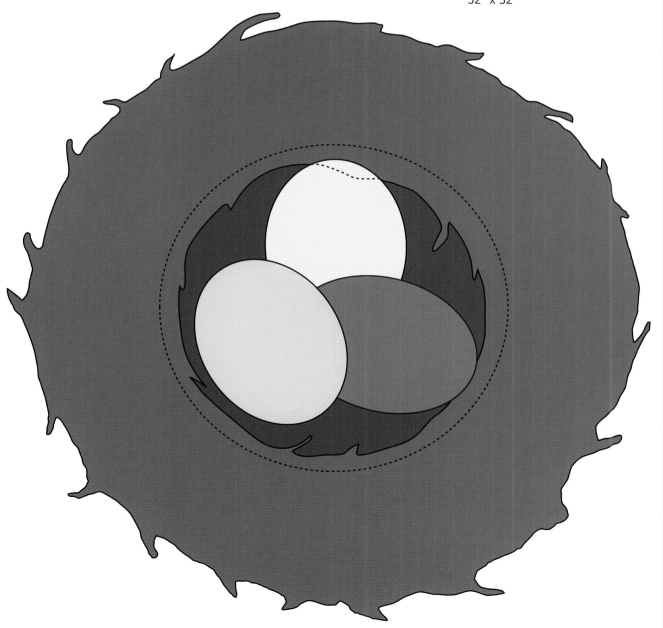

# Tree Rings
# TABLE RUNNER

## Making the Table Runner

1. Refer to Quick Corner Triangles on page 108. Making quick corner triangle units, sew four 6" Fabric C squares to one 11½" Fabric A square as shown. Press. Make two.

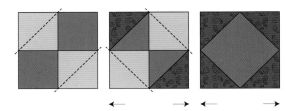

Fabric C = 6 x 6
Fabric A = 11½ x 11½
Make 2

2. Making quick corner triangle units, sew four 6" Fabric C squares to one 11½" Fabric B square as shown. Press.

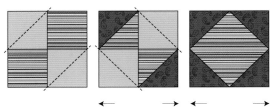

Fabric C = 6 x 6
Fabric B = 11½ x 11½

3. Sew unit from step 2 between two units from step 1. Press.

4. Sew two ¾" x 33½" Border strips to top and bottom of unit from step 3. Press seams toward border.

5. Sew two ¾" x 12" Border strips to sides of unit from step 4. Press seams toward border.

| Tree Rings Table Runner Finished Size: 12½" x 34½" | FIRST CUT | | SECOND CUT | |
|---|---|---|---|---|
| | Number of Strips or Pieces | Dimensions | Number of Pieces | Dimensions |
| **Fabric A** Appliqué Background ⅜ yard | 1 | 11½" x 42" | 2 | 11½" squares |
| **Fabric B** Appliqué Background ⅜ yard | 1 | 11½" x 42" | 1 | 11½" square |
| **Fabric C** Background ½ yard | 2 | 6" x 42" | 12 | 6" squares |
| **Border** ⅛ yard | 3 | ¾" x 42" | 2 / 2 | ¾" x 33½" / ¾" x 12" |
| **Binding** ⅓ yard | 3 | 2¾" x 42" | | |
| 7" Circle Appliqué - ¼ yard 4" Circle Appliqué - Scrap each of 2 fabrics Backing - ½ yard Batting - 17" x 39" Lightweight Fusible Web - ⅔ yard | | | | |

## Fabric Requirements and Cutting Instructions

Read all instructions before beginning and use ¼"-wide seam allowances throughout. Read Cutting Strips and Pieces on page 108 prior to cutting fabric.

## Getting Started

Stylish and graphic elements make this table runner a great accent for any home decor. Block measures 11½" square (unfinished). Refer to Accurate Seam Allowance on page 108. Whenever possible use Assembly Line Method on page 108. Press seams in direction of arrows.

Like rings in a tree, this table runner symbolizes stability, stature, and new growth.
Three blocks are placed on point to hold the captivating circle shapes on this small runner.
A striped binding becomes an important design element with this color combination.

## Adding the Appliqués

Refer to appliqué instructions on page 109. Our instructions are for Quick-Fuse Appliqué, but if you prefer hand appliqué add ¼"-wide seam allowances.

1. Use patterns on page 111 to trace three 7" circles and three 4" circles on paper side of fusible web. Use appropriate fabrics to prepare all appliqués for fusing.

2. Refer to photo and layout to position and fuse appliqués to quilt. Finish appliqué edges with machine satin stitch or other decorative stitching as desired.

## Layering and Finishing

1. Referring to Layering the Quilt on page 110, arrange and baste backing, batting, and top together. Hand or machine quilt as desired.

2. Refer to Binding the Quilt on page 110. Use 2¾"-wide Binding strips to bind quilt.

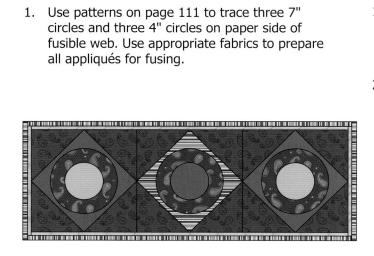

### Tree Rings TABLE RUNNER
Finished Size: 12½" x 34½"

# Nesting Instinct PILLOW

Beautiful and textural, this wool pillow will be an eye-catching favorite.

## Materials Needed

Background Pieces - See page 16

Backing - ½ yard
  Two 9" x 12½" pieces

Appliqués - Assorted wool scraps

Lightweight Fusible Web - ⅓ yard

Interfacing (Fusible or Sew-in) - ⅓ yard

12" Pillow Form
  OR Optional Pillow Form - ½ yard
    Two 12½" Fabric Squares
    Polyester Fiberfill

## Fabric Requirements and Cutting Instructions

When purchasing fabric, see page 16 for Nesting Instinct 2-Piece Quilt, for Fabrics B, C, D, and E and additional materials listed on this page. Read all instructions before beginning and use ¼"-wide seam allowances throughout. Read Cutting Strips and Pieces on page 108 prior to cutting fabric.

## Making the Pillow

Refer to Nesting Instinct 2-Piece Quilt chart, and Making the Smaller Quilt, on page 16. Cut fabrics B, C, D, and E as listed in chart. These pieces need to be backed with interfacing to help prevent stretching and give body to the fabric. Refer to appliqué instructions on page 109. Our instructions are for Quick-Fuse Appliqué, but if you prefer hand appliqué, reverse patterns and add ¼"-wide seam allowances for cotton fabrics.

1.  Starting with step 3 on page 16, follow instructions through step 7 to construct pillow top and add appliqués.

## Finishing the Pillow

1.  Use two 9" x 12½" Backing pieces and refer to Finishing Pillows, page 111 steps 2-4, to sew backing.

2.  Insert 12" pillow form or refer to Pillow Forms on page 111 to make a pillow form if desired.

**Nesting Instinct PILLOW**
Finished Size: 12" x 12"

# Natural Elements TRAY

**Personalize and beautify a purchased wicker tray by adding your own mosaic design.**

## Materials Needed

**Slate and Glass Tiles** - Various sizes and shapes. Tiles should all be the same depth. (We used left-over pieces from other projects and purchased a few tile border pieces [listello] from a home improvement store.)

**Smooth Rocks** - Any size; must be same depth as tile.

**Founds Objects or Collectibles** - Metal Shapes, large beads, etc.

**Wicker or Wooden Tray with Flat Bottom**

**Tile Adhesive or Clear Adhesive Caulk**

**Non-Sanded Grout, Rubber Grout Float, Grout Sponge, Bucket**

**Stone Tile Gloss Sealer**

**Masking Tape**

## Making the Tray

1. Using photo as inspiration, arrange mosaic items in bottom of tray leaving small spaces (⅛") between objects for grout. Note: Tile borders may be mounted on mesh; cut pieces off as desired, or peel off the mesh backing. All items should be about the same depth so that tray will be serviceable.

2. When satisfied with the design, use tile adhesive or caulk to glue each piece to tray bottom. Glue one piece at a time to maintain arrangement. If needed, build up found objects with layers of adhesive to achieve an even depth with surrounding tiles. Following adhesive manufacturer's directions for drying time, allow to dry thoroughly.

3. Use masking tape to mask off wicker portions of tray. Following manufacturer's directions, grout mosaic arrangement. Remove masking tape before grout dries.

4. Following manufacturer's directions, apply sealer to stones and slate tiles.

Gather the family in a kitchen that's glowing with color, personality, and charm. Clever quilts decorate the walls and table creating a space that draws everyone into its welcoming warmth.

# Gathering
# PLACES

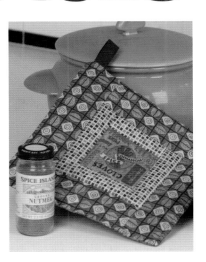

# Apple Box WALL QUILT

Half the boxes are full in this striking pieced tribute to a favorite fruit. Deep rich colors combine with a clever construction technique to make this Fat Quarter fabrication.

| Apple Box Wall Quilt Finished Size: 27½" x 43½" | FIRST CUT | |
|---|---|---|
| | Number of Pieces | Dimensions |
| **Fabric A - Assorted Reds** | | |
| A1 Fat Quarter | 3 | 2½" x 4½" |
| | 10 | 2½" squares |
| A2 Fat Quarter | 3 | 2½" x 4½" |
| | 8 | 2½" squares |
| | 3 | 1½" squares |
| A3 Fat Quarter | 2 | 2½" x 4½" |
| | 12 | 2½" squares |
| | 3 | 1½" squares |
| A4 Fat Quarter | 5 | 2½" squares |
| A5 Fat Quarter | 5 | 2½" x 4½" |
| | 5 | 2½" squares |
| **Fabric B - Assorted Greens** | | |
| B1 Fat Quarter | 3 | 2½" x 4½" |
| | 6 | 2½" squares |
| | 2 | 1½" squares |
| | 2 | 1" squares |
| B2 Fat Quarter | 5 | 2½" x 4½" |
| | 10 | 2½" squares |
| B3 Fat Quarter | 5 | 2½" x 4½" |
| | 5 | 2½" squares |
| B4 Fat Quarter | 2 | 2½" x 4½" |
| | 5 | 2½" squares |
| B5 Fat Quarter | 2 | 2½" x 4½" |
| | 9 | 2½" squares |
| | 3 | 1½" squares |
| | 3 | 1" squares |
| B6 Fat Quarter | 3 | 2½" x 4½" |
| | 3 | 2½" squares |
| | 3 | 1" squares |

| Apple Box Wall Quilt CONTINUED | FIRST CUT | |
|---|---|---|
| | Number of Pieces | Dimensions |
| **Fabric C - Assorted Browns** | | |
| C1 Fat Quarter | 2 | 2½" x 4½" |
| | 5 | 2½" squares |
| | 3 | 1½" squares |
| C2 Fat Quarter | 10 | 2½" x 4½" |
| | 10 | 2½" squares |
| C3 Fat Quarter | 3 | 2½" x 4½" |
| | 6 | 2½" squares |
| | 3 | 1½" squares |
| **Fabric D - Assorted Golds/Tans** | | |
| D1 Fat Quarter | 6 | 2½" x 4½" |
| | 8 | 2½" squares |
| | 8 | 1½" squares |
| | 5 | 1" squares |
| D2 Fat Quarter | 2 | 2½" x 4½" |
| | 5 | 2½" squares |
| | 2 | 1½" squares |
| | 3 | 1" squares |
| D3 Fat Quarter | 2 | 2½" x 4½" |
| | 4 | 2½" squares |
| | 5 | 1½" squares |
| Fabric E Orange Fat Quarter | 2 | 2½" x 4½" |
| | 4 | 2½" squares |
| 1st Border ⅙ yard | 4 | 1" x 42" |
| Outside Border ¼ yard | 4 | 1¼" x 42" |
| Binding ⅜ yard | 4 | 2¾" x 42" |

Appliqué Leaves - Scraps
Backing - 1⅜ yards
Batting - 32" x 48"
Lightweight Fusible Web - Scraps

# Fabric Requirements and Cutting Instructions

Read all instructions before beginning and use ¼"-wide seam allowances throughout. Read Cutting Strips and Pieces on page 108 prior to cutting fabric.

## Getting Started

Multi-colored blocks surround our scrumptious apples in this distinctive wall quilt. Blocks measure 8½" square (unfinished). Refer to Accurate Seam Allowance on page 108. Whenever possible use Assembly Line Method on page 108. Press seams in direction of arrows.

## Making Multi-Patch Blocks (1, 2 & 3)

1. Sew one 2½" Fabric A5 square to one 2½" Fabric D3 square as shown. Press. Sew this unit to one 2½" x 4½" Fabric A5 piece. Press. Make two.

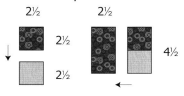

Make 2
(Fabric A5/D3)

2. Refer to step 1 to arrange and sew two units each in the following fabric combinations: 2½" x 4½" Fabric E piece, 2½" Fabric E square, and 2½" Fabric B5 square; 2½" x 4½" Fabric C1 piece, 2½" Fabric C1 square, and 2½" Fabric A3 square; 2½" x 4½" Fabric B4 piece, 2½" Fabric B4 square, and 2½" Fabric D1 square.

Make 2            Make 2
(Fabric E/B5)     (Fabric C1/A3)

Make 2
(Fabric B4/D1)

3. Sew one A5/D3 unit to one E/B5 unit as shown. Press. Make two. Sew one C1/A3 unit to one B4/D1 unit. Press. Make two.

Make 2  ←

Make 2  →

4. Sew two units from step 3, one of each combination, together as shown. Refer to Twisting Seams on page 108. Press. Make two. Block 1 measures 8½" square.

**Block 1**

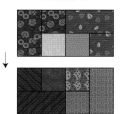

Make 2
Block measures 8½" square

5. Refer to step 1 to arrange and sew three units each in the following fabric combinations: 2½" x 4½" Fabric B2 piece, 2½" Fabric B2 square, and 2½" Fabric D2 square; 2½" x 4½" Fabric A2 piece, 2½" Fabric A2 square, and 2½" Fabric C1 square; 2½" x 4½" Fabric D1 piece, 2½" Fabric D1 square, and 2½" Fabric C3 square; 2½" x 4½" Fabric B6 piece, 2½" Fabric B6 square, and 2½" Fabric A3 square.

Make 3            Make 3
(Fabric B2/D2)    (Fabric A2/C1)

Make 3            Make 3
(Fabric D1/C3)    (Fabric B6/A3)

**Apple Box Wall Quilt**

Tracing Line  _____

Leaves
Make 8

6. Sew one B2/D2 unit to one A2/C1 unit as shown. Press. Make three. Sew one D1/C3 unit to one B6/A3 unit. Press. Make three. Sew two units from this step, one of each combination, together as shown. Twist seams. Press. Make three. Block 2 measures 8½" square.

**Block 2**

Make 6
(3 of each combination)

Make 3
Block measures 8½" square

7. Refer to step 1 to arrange and sew two units each in the following fabric combinations: 2½" x 4½" Fabric C2 piece, 2½" Fabric C2 square, and 2½" Fabric B5 square; 2½" x 4½" Fabric D3 piece, 2½" Fabric D3 square, and 2½" Fabric E square; 2½" x 4½" Fabric B3 piece, 2½" Fabric B3 square, and 2½" Fabric A1 square; 2½" x 4½" Fabric A3 piece, 2½" Fabric A3 square, and 2½" Fabric B2 square.

Make 2
(Fabric C2/B5)

Make 2
(Fabric D3/E)

Make 2
(Fabric B3/A1)

Make 2
(Fabric A3/B2)

8. Sew one C2/B5 unit to one D3/E unit as shown. Press. Make two. Sew one B3/A1 unit to one A3/B2 unit. Press. Make two. Sew two units from this step, one of each combination, together as shown. Twist seams. Press. Make two. Block 3 measures 8½" square.

**Block 3**

Make 4
(2 of each combination)

Make 2
Block measures 8½" square

## Making the Apple Blocks

1. Refer to Quick Corner Triangles on page 108. Making quick corner triangle units, sew one 1½" Fabric D3 square and one 1" Fabric B1 square to one 2½" Fabric A3 square as shown. Press. Make two.

Fabric D3 = 1½ x 1½
Fabric B1 = 1 x 1
Fabric A3 = 2½ x 2½
Make 2

2. Sew one 2½" Fabric C2 square to one unit from step 1 as shown. Press. Sew one 2½" x 4½" Fabric C2 piece to this unit. Press. Make two and label Unit 1.

**Unit 1**

2½     2½

2½          4½

Make 2

3. Making quick corner triangle units, sew one 1" Fabric D1 square and one 1½" Fabric D2 square to one 2½" Fabric A1 square as shown. Press. Make two.

Fabric D1 = 1 x 1
Fabric D2 = 1½ x 1½
Fabric A1 = 2½ x 2½
Make 2

4. Sew one 2½" Fabric B2 square to one unit from step 3 as shown. Press. Sew one 2½" x 4½" Fabric B2 piece to this unit as shown. Press. Make two and label Unit 2.

**Unit 2**

2½          4½

2½          2½

Make 2

5. Making quick corner triangle unit, sew one 1½" Fabric D1 square to one 2½" Fabric A2 square as shown. Press. Make two.

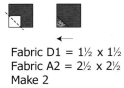

Fabric D1 = 1½ x 1½
Fabric A2 = 2½ x 2½
Make 2

6. Sew one 2½" Fabric B5 square to one unit from step 5 as shown. Press. Sew one 2½" x 4½" Fabric B5 piece to this unit. Press. Make two and label Unit 3.

**Unit 3**

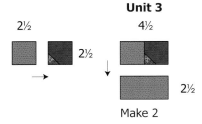

Make 2

7. Making quick corner triangle unit, sew one 1½" Fabric B1 square to one 2½" Fabric A4 square as shown. Press. Make two.

Fabric B1 = 1½ x 1½
Fabric A4 = 2½ x 2½
Make 2

8. Sew one 2½" Fabric D2 square to one unit from step 7 as shown. Press. Sew one 2½" x 4½" Fabric D2 piece to this unit. Press. Make two and label Unit 4.

**Unit 4**

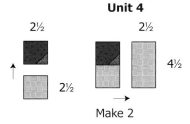

Make 2

9. Arrange and sew one of each Unit 1, 2, 3, and 4 together as shown. Twist seams. Press. Make two. Block 4 measures 8½" square.

**Block 4**

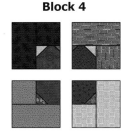

Make 2
Block measures 8½" square

10. Refer to steps 1 and 2 to sew Unit 1. Sew quick corner triangle units using 1½" Fabric C3 square and 1" Fabric D1 square to one 2½" Fabric B1 square. Sew this unit to one 2½" Fabric A1 square and one 2½" x 4½" Fabric A1 pieces. Press. Make three.

**Unit 1**

Make 3

11. Refer to steps 3 and 4 to sew Unit 2. Sew quick corner triangle units using 1" Fabric B6 square and 1½" Fabric A2 square to one 2½" Fabric B5 square. Sew this unit to one 2½" Fabric C2 square and one 2½" x 4½" Fabric C2 piece. Press. Make three.

**Unit 2**

Make 3

12. Refer to steps 5 and 6 to sew Unit 3. Sew quick corner triangle unit using 1½" Fabric A3 square to one 2½" Fabric B4 square. Sew this unit to one 2½" Fabric D1 square and one 2½" x 4½" Fabric D1 piece. Press. Make three.

**Unit 3**

Make 3

13. Refer to steps 7 and 8 to sew Unit 4. Sew quick corner triangle unit using 1½" Fabric C1 square to one 2½" Fabric B2 square. Sew this unit to one 2½" Fabric A5 square and one 2½" x 4½" Fabric A5 piece. Press. Make three.

**Unit 4**

Make 3

14. Arrange and sew one of each Unit 1, 2, 3, and 4 together as shown. Twist seams. Press. Make three. Block 5 measures 8½" square.

**Block 5**

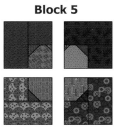

Make 3
Block measures 8½" square

15. Refer to steps 1 and 2 to sew Unit 1. Sew quick corner triangle units using 1½" Fabric D3 square and 1" Fabric D2 square to one 2½" Fabric A2 square. Sew this unit to one 2½" Fabric B1 square and one 2½" x 4½" Fabric B1 piece. Press. Make three.

**Unit 1**

Make 3

16. Refer to steps 3 and 4 to sew Unit 2. Sew quick corner triangle units using 1" Fabric B5 square and 1½" Fabric D1 square to one 2½" Fabric A3 square. Sew this unit to one 2½" Fabric C3 square and one 2½" x 4½" Fabric C3 piece. Press. Make three.

**Unit 2**

Make 3

17. Refer to steps 5 and 6 to sew Unit 3. Sew quick corner triangle unit using 1½" Fabric D1 square to one 2½" Fabric A1 square. Sew this unit to one 2½" Fabric C2 square and one 2½" x 4½" Fabric C2 piece. Press. Make three.

**Unit 3**

Make 3

18. Refer to steps 7 and 8 to sew Unit 4. Sew quick corner triangle unit using 1½" Fabric B5 square to one 2½" Fabric A4 square. Sew this unit to one 2½" Fabric B3 square and one 2½" x 4½" Fabric B3 piece. Press. Make three.

**Unit 4**

Make 3

19. Arrange and sew one of each Unit 1, 2, 3, and 4 together as shown. Twist seams. Press. Make three. Block 6 measures 8½" square.

**Block 6**

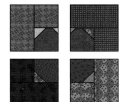

Make 3
Block measures 8½" square

## Adding the Appliqués

Refer to appliqué instructions on page 109. Our instructions are for Quick-Fuse Appliqué, but if you prefer hand appliqué add ¼"-wide seam allowances.

1. Use pattern on page 30 to trace eight leaves on paper side of fusible web. Use appropriate fabrics to prepare all appliqués for fusing.

2. Refer to photo on page 29 to position and fuse appliqués to quilt. Finish appliqué edges with machine satin stitch or other decorative stitching as desired.

## Assembling the Quilt

1. Referring to photo on page 29, arrange Blocks into rows. Rows consist of the following combinations. Row 1 uses Blocks 1, 4, and 5; Row 2 uses Blocks 6, 2, and 3; Row 3 uses Blocks 5, 3, and 4; Row 4 uses Blocks 2, 6, and 5; Row 5 uses Blocks 6, 1, and 2.

2. Sew blocks into rows pressing seams in opposite direction from row to row. Sew rows together. Press.

3. Refer to Adding the Borders on page 110. Measure quilt through center from side to side. Cut two 1"-wide First Border strips to this measurement. Sew to top and bottom of quilt. Press seams toward border.

4. Sew 1" x 42" First Border strips together end-to-end to make one continuous 1"-wide First Border strip. Measure quilt through center from top to bottom including borders just added. Cut two 1"-wide First Border strips to this measurement. Sew to sides of quilt. Press.

5. Refer to steps 3 and 4 to join, measure, trim, and sew 1¼"-wide Outside Border strips to top, bottom, and sides of quilt. Press.

## Layering and Finishing

1. Referring to Layering the Quilt on page 110, arrange and baste backing, batting, and top together. Hand or machine quilt as desired.

2. Refer to Binding the Quilt on page 110. Sew 2¾" x 42" binding strips end-to-end to make one continuous 2¾"-wide binding strip. Bind quilt to finish.

# Orchard Stripes
# WINDOW VALANCE

## Fabric Requirements and Cutting Instructions

Read all instructions before beginning and use ¼"-wide seam allowances throughout. Read Cutting Strips and Pieces on page 108 prior to cutting fabric.

## Getting Started

Rich harvest colors were selected for our valance but could easily be made with any color combination. This valance does not have a rod pocket instead it was hung with drapery clips. Our window measures 30" and the finished valance size measures 14" x 62½". Add or subtract fabric strips to adjust valance width to your window opening. Press seams in direction of arrows.

## Making the Valance

1. Refer to diagram below to arrange and sew the following strips: two 3½" x 14½" and two 2" x 14½" Fabric A, one 3" x 14½" and two 2" x 14½" Fabric B, one 3½" x 14½", two 3" x 14½" and two 2" x 14½" Fabric C, one 3" x 14½" and three 2" x 14½" Fabric D, one 3" x 14½", one 2" x 14½" and one 1½" x 14½" Fabric E, one 3½" x 14½", two 3" x 14½", one 2" x 14½" and one 1½" x 14½" Fabric F, two 3" x 14½" and two 2" x 14½" Fabric G, and two 3" x 14½" and one 2" x 14½" Fabric H. Press.

| Orchard Stripes Window Valance Finished Size: 14" x 62½" | FIRST CUT | |
|---|---|---|
| | Number of Strips or Pieces | Dimensions |
| Fabric A Fat Quarter | 2 | 3½" x 14½" |
| | 2 | 2" x 14½" |
| Fabric B Fat Quarter | 1 | 3" x 14½" |
| | 2 | 2" x 14½" |
| Fabric C Fat Quarter | 1 | 3½" x 14½" |
| | 2 | 3" x 14½" |
| | 2 | 2" x 14½" |
| Fabric D Fat Quarter | 1 | 3" x 14½" |
| | 3 | 2" x 14½" |
| Fabric E Fat Quarter | 1 | 3" x 14½" |
| | 1 | 2" x 14½" |
| | 1 | 1½" x 14½" |
| Fabric F Fat Quarter | 1 | 3½" x 14½" |
| | 2 | 3" x 14½" |
| | 1 | 2" x 14½" |
| | 1 | 1½" x 14½" |
| Fabric G Fat Quarter | 2 | 3" x 14½" |
| | 2 | 2" x 14½" |
| Fabric H Fat Quarter | 2 | 3" x 14½" |
| | 1 | 2" x 14½" |
| Backing - 1 yard Drapery Clips | | |

3½  3  2  2  3  2  2  3  2  3  3½  2  3  3  2  3½  3  3½  2  1½ 2 1½  3  2  2  2  2  3  3  3

14½

Stripes in various widths join together to mimic the rich landscape of an orchard in autumn on this eye-catching window treatment. Instead of the usual rod pocket, we chose to use wall hooks and drapery clips for an unconventional finish.

2.  Cut backing lengthwise into two equal pieces. Sew pieces together to make one 20" x 72" (approximate) backing piece. Press.

3.  Measure pieced unit from step 1 and cut backing fabric to this measurement.

4.  Place pieced unit and backing piece right sides together. Using ¼"-wide seam, stitch around all edges, leaving a 5" opening on one side for turning. Clip corners, turn, and press. Hand-stitch opening closed.

5.  Hang valance using drapery clips.

# Apple Stacks WALL QUILT

## Making the Wall Quilt

1. Arrange and sew together two 5¼" x 36" Fabric B strips, four 1¼" x 36" Fabric C strips, two 5½" x 36" Fabric A strips, and one 1" x 36" Fabric B strip as shown. Press.

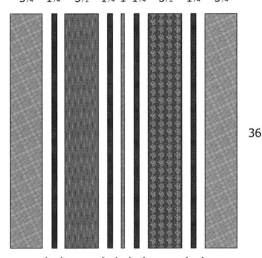

| Apple Stacks Wall Quilt Finished Size: 16" x 28" | FIRST CUT | | SECOND CUT | |
|---|---|---|---|---|
| | Number of Strips or Pieces | Dimensions | Number of Pieces | Dimensions |
| **Fabric A** Appliqué Background ¼ yard each of 2 Fabrics | 1* | 5½" x 42" *cut for each fabric | 1* | 5½" x 36" |
| **Fabric B** Light Accent ⅜ yard | 2 1 | 5¼" x 42" 1" x 42" | 2 1 | 5¼" x 36" 1" x 36" |
| **Fabric C** Dark Accent ¼ yard | 4 | 1¼" x 42" | 4 | 1¼" x 36" |

Appliqué Apples - Fat Quarter or scraps (each of 6 fabrics)
Appliqué Leaves & Stems - Assorted scraps
Backing - ¾ yard
Batting - 27" x 40"
Lightweight Fusible Web - 1 yard
Photo Transfer Paper and/or Fabric
Frame 16" x 28" or two 16" & two 28" Stretcher Bars
Removable Fabric Marker

## Fabric Requirements and Cutting Instructions

Read all instructions before beginning and use ¼"-wide seam allowances throughout. Read Cutting Strips and Pieces on page 108 prior to cutting fabric.

## Getting Started

This wall quilt wraps around a frame and is accented with photo transferred apple cores that are placed on a few selected apples. Use ¼"-wide seam allowances for this project.

2. Using a removable fabric marker, draw a 16" x 28" rectangle on unit from step 1, centering it as shown below. This will be used as a placement guide for appliqué apples.

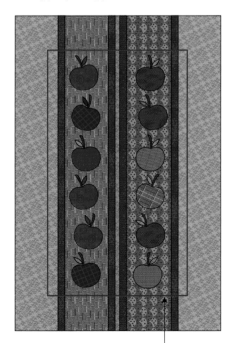

Frame Placement

Apples stack one on top of the other in this ingenious wall art. Use our artwork and a photo transfer method to "cut" some apples in half, exposing their core. Try stretching the wallhanging on a wooden frame for a different look or bind as desired.

## Adding the Appliqués

Refer to appliqué instructions on page 109. Our instructions are for Quick-Fuse Appliqué, but if you prefer hand appliqué add ¼"-wide seam allowances. Note: Both regular and reversed patterns are given below.

1. Use patterns below to trace twelve of apples, stems, and leaves on paper side of fusible web. Use appropriate fabrics to prepare all appliqués for fusing.

2. Refer to photo on page 37 and step 2 diagram on page 36 to position and fuse appliqués to quilt.

3. Use Apple Core pattern below for photo transfer. Refer to manufacturer's instruction to copy five apple cores onto photo transfer paper and/or photo transfer fabric, and set colors as instructed. Apple cores are presented as both original and reversed images. Use the core appropriate for your photo transfer method.

4. Fuse web to wrong side of apple core unit from step 3. Cut out apple core along design's outside line. Refer to photo on page 37 to fuse apple cores to selected apples.

5. Finish appliqué edges with machine satin stitch or other decorative stitching as desired.

## Finishing the Wall Quilt

1. Referring to Layering the Quilt on page 110, arrange and baste backing, batting, and top together. Hand or machine quilt as desired.

2. Refer to Create Wall Art, Making the Wall Art on page 100. Attach quilt to frame using either 16" x 28" frame or two 16" and two 28" stretcher bars.

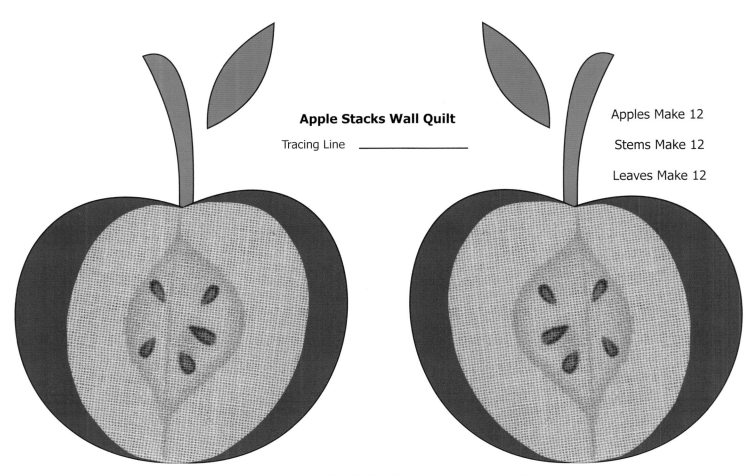

**Apple Stacks Wall Quilt**

Tracing Line  _____

Apples Make 12

Stems Make 12

Leaves Make 12

*Permission is granted by Debbie Mumm Inc. to copy page 38
to successfully complete the Apple Stacks Wall Quilt.*

# Apple Box
# CHAIR CUSHIONS

Extend the beauty of our apple box block to your chairs by making cushions or covers for your chairs.

## Fabric Requirements and Cutting Instructions

Read all instructions before beginning and use ¼"-wide seam allowances throughout. Read Cutting Strips and Pieces on page 108 prior to cutting fabric.

## Making the Chair Cushion

Remove and measure seat from chair. Adjust Fabric D strips to accommodate your chair size. Our chair seat measured 18" square. Fabric width is cut allowing it to wrap around chair seat, pulled to underneath side and attached.

## Materials Needed
### FOR ONE CUSHION

Fabric A (Center) - Scrap
(each of 4 fabrics)
    One 2½" square

Fabric B (1st Accent) - Scrap
(each of 4 fabrics)
    One 2½" x 4½"
    One 2½" square

Fabric C (2nd Accent) - Scrap
(each of 4 fabrics)
    One 2½" x 6½"
    One 2½" x 4½"

Fabric D (Outside Accent) - ⅓ yard
(each of 4 fabrics*)
    One 8½" x 14½"
    One 8½" x 6½"

Lining - ⅓ yard (will not show)
    One 32" x 32"

Batting - 32" x 32"

*Note: Adjust Fabric D sizes to fit chair.

1. Refer to Multi-Patch Blocks instructions on page 30 steps 1 and 2. Using Fabric A and B pieces make four, one in each combination.

2. Using same procedure as step 1, sew one 2½" x 4½" and 2½" x 6½" Fabric C pieces to unit. Press. Sew one 8½" x 6½" and 8½" x 14½" Fabric D pieces to unit. Press. Make four, one of each combination. Refer to photo to sew units together. Press.

3. Refer to Layering the Quilt on page 110 to prepare cushion for quilting. Quilt as desired.

4. Center quilted seat cover on top of chair cushion. Pull sides snugly to the back temporarily placing one staple on each side. Check front to see if the outside edge is even on all sides. Adjust if needed. Continue stapling sides and corners, pulling fabric snugly. Install seat chair in chair frame.

# Coffee Break TABLE RUNNER

| Coffee Break Table Runner Finished Size: 15" x 57" | FIRST CUT | | SECOND CUT | |
|---|---|---|---|---|
| | Number of Strips or Pieces | Dimensions | Number of Pieces | Dimensions |
| Fabric A 1⅝ yards | 1 | 56½" x 42"* | 1 2 | 56½" x 5½" 56½" x 1" |
| Fabric B ⅓ yard | 3 3 | 1½" x 42" 1" x 42" | | |
| Fabric C ⅙ yard | 3 | 1" x 42" | | |
| Fabric D 1⅝ yards | 1 | 56½" x 42"* | 2 | 56½" x 2½" |
| Binding ⅜ yard | 4 | 2¾" x 42" | | |
| Backing - ⅞ yard Batting - 19" x 61" *The fabric strip used in the tablerunner will be seamless. | | | | |

## Fabric Requirements and Cutting Instructions

Read all instructions before beginning and use ¼"-wide seam allowances throughout. Read Cutting Strips and Pieces on page 108 prior to cutting fabric.

## Getting Started

This simple to make table runner is a great way to accent a table for everyday or for a evening with family and friends. Make several using colors inspired by the seasons or holidays.

## Making the Table Runner

1. Sew 1½" x 42" Fabric B strips together end-to-end to make one continuous 1½"-wide Fabric B strip. Cut two 1½" x 56½" strips from this piece. Repeat step to sew, measure and cut, 1"-wide Fabric B strips and 1"-wide Fabric C strips.

2. Arrange and sew together two 56½" x 2½" Fabric D strips, two 56½" x 1" Fabric A strips, two 1" x 56½" Fabric B strips, two 1" x 56½" Fabric C strips, two 1½" x 56½" Fabric B strips, and one 56½" x 5½" Fabric A strips as shown. Press.

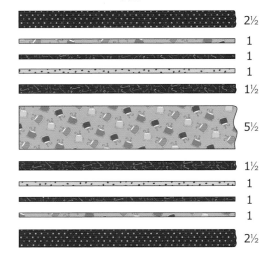

3. Cut backing lengthwise into two equal pieces. Sew pieces together crosswise to make one 20" x 63" (approximate) backing piece. Press.

4. Referring to Layering the Quilt on page 110, arrange and baste backing, batting, and top together. Hand or machine quilt as desired.

5. Refer to Binding the Quilt on page 110. Sew 2¾" x 42" binding strips end-to-end to make one continuous 2¾"-wide binding strip. Bind quilt to finish.

## Making the Napkins

Be ready for a casual meal or coffee by stocking a festive tin container with pretty napkins, silverware, and flowers.

Cut one 18½" square and two 1" x 17½" strips and two 1" x 18½" strips from a motif fabric and one 17½" square from a coordinate. Using ¼"-wide seams with right sides together, sew 1" x 17½" motif strips to top and bottom of 17½" square. Sew 1" x 18½" motif strips to sides including borders just added. Press. With right sides together, sew pieced unit and 18½" motif square on all sides, leaving a 4" opening for turning. Clip corners, turn, and press. Hand-stitch opening closed.

Coffee and kitchens just seem to go together and this table runner invites you to relax, enjoy a cup of coffee or tea, and visit with family and friends. Simple stripes make this runner so fast and fun to sew that you'll want to extend your sewing time by making matching napkins.

# Coffee Dotty
# APRON

| Coffee Dotty Apron | FIRST CUT | |
| --- | --- | --- |
| | Number of Strips or Pieces | Dimensions |
| 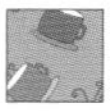 Apron Front<br>⅞ yard | 1 | 26½" x 26" |
| Lining<br>⅞ yard | 1 | 26½" x 26" |
|  Ruffle, Pockets,<br>Waist Ties,<br>Neck Ties &<br>Apron Accents<br>1⅛ yards | 1<br>4<br>2<br>2<br>2 | 10½" x 38½"<br>6½" squares<br>5¼" x 28½"<br>5¼" x 19½"<br>1½" x 12" |
| Pocket Center - Motif scrap<br>  Two 4" squares<br>Rickrack Trim - 1 yard<br>Fusible Web - Scrap | | |

## Getting Started

Let's have some fun in the kitchen by entertaining in style with this cute "Café" apron.

## Making the Apron

1. Trace armhole curve pattern (page 44) on 8½" x 11" piece of paper. Fold 26½" x 26" Apron Front piece in half crosswise (folded piece measures 13¼" x 26"). Align pattern on top corner edges, pin, and cut out arm curve. Stay-stitch curved edge. Repeat step to cut curve for 26½" x 26" Lining piece.

2. Press one short end of 5¼" x 28½" Waist Tie piece ¼" to the wrong side. Fold ties in half lengthwise and press. Open and fold raw edges to center pressed line. Press. Fold again in half lengthwise. Press. Top stitch folds in place (two long and one short side) of tie. Make two.

3. Repeat step 2 to fold, press, and topstitch two 5¼" x 19½" Neck Tie pieces.

4. Fold one 1½" x 12" Apron Accent piece ¼" to the wrong side along both long sides. Press. Make two.

5. Refer to photo to arrange and pin folded accent pieces from step 4 and rickrack trim to top section of apron as desired. Place first trim ½" away from top cut edge as this will keep it away from top seam allowance area. Stitch to apron. Trim to match curved apron edges.

6. Place and pin neck ties ⅜" from curved top edges. Baste in place. Pin ties in center of apron to keep them away from outside edges.

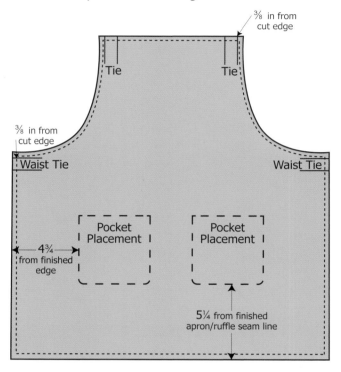

7. Place and pin waist ties ⅜" from apron lower curved edge. Baste in place. Pin ties in center of apron to keep them away from outside edges.

8. Fold 10½" x 38½" Ruffle strip in half lengthwise right sides together and stitch side edges. Clip corners, turn and press. Baste raw edges together.

9. With right-sides-together, pin ruffle to bottom edge of apron front. Make ½" tucks across ruffle every 2¼" – 2½", spacing evenly across ruffle. Baste in place. Pin ruffle to center of apron to keep it away from outside edges.

10. Place apron and lining pieces right-sides-together. Using ¼"-wide seam, stitch around all edges, leaving a 7" opening on one side for turning. Clip corners, turn, and press. Hand-stitch opening closed.

Aprons are all the rage and this one shows you why!
Rickrack, pockets, and a flirty ruffle make this apron
adorable. Or, turn the other side out and enjoy the
pretty repeating stripe print. You'll want to wear this
apron everyday.

11. Refer to appliqué instructions on page 109 to prepare 4" fussy-cut motif square for appliquéing. Round bottom edges referring to photo. Use appropriate fabrics to prepare all appliqués for fusing. Center motif on one 6½" Apron pocket square and fuse in place. Finish appliqué edges with machine satin stitch or other decorative stitching as desired. Make two.

12. Place unit from step 11 and 6½" Pocket-backing piece right-sides-together. Round bottom corners of pockets. Using ¼"-wide seam, stitch around all edges, leaving an opening on one side for turning. Clip corners, turn, and press. Hand-stitch opening closed. Make two.

13. Refer to photo to arrange pocket on apron approximately 4¾" from finished side edges and 5¼" from bottom apron/ruffle seam line. Topstitch bottom and side edges of pocket reinforcing stitches at top edges.

14. Top-stitch ¼" away from apron outside edges.

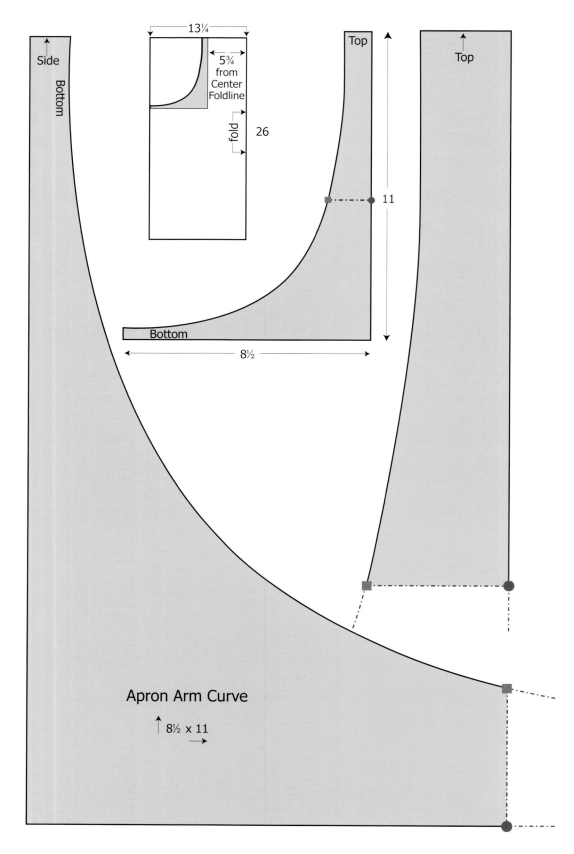

Apron Arm Curve

8½ x 11

# It's in the details

Apples and coffee decorate the kitchen in this book, but many more themes and color schemes can be used. Your room décor can be inspired by a season, a decorating style, or a favorite thing or activity. Look for inspiration in a favorite fabric collection and all the room's accessories will be easy to design.

**Coffee House**

COFFEE is a natural for the kitchen and the turquoise and green colors add a robust twist to traditional coffee colors. For a complete kitchen ensemble adapt our apple quilts by replacing the apples with appliquéd coffee cups.

**Spice of Life**

If you love to bake, SPICE might be the perfect ingredient for a savory kitchen. Tangy colors and stylized patterns combine with spice-sprinkled motifs to cook up a flavorful decorating scheme. Use fussy-cut motifs to replace the apples on our Apple Box Wall Quilt for a zesty substitution.

Add flair and raise your culinary status from cook to TOP CHEF by decorating the kitchen in a fanciful chef theme. Lobsters, veggies, utensils, pots and pans, and chef hats are some of the fun motifs to feature in your fabric projects. Change the apples on the Apple Box Wall Quilt into red and green peppers by making twice as many of the apple top units and using them on top and bottom to make a pepper shape.

**Top Chef**

Create bright and beautiful outdoor living spaces with quilts and accessories perfect for easy-going warm weather relaxation.

# Outdoor RETREATS

# Sunny Side Up LAP QUILT

## Fabric Requirements and Cutting Instructions

Read all instructions before beginning and use ¼"-wide seam allowances throughout. Read Cutting Strips and Pieces on page 108 prior to cutting fabric.

## Getting Started

Colors of the great outdoors are showcased in this easy to make quilt. Each block measures 11½" square (unfinished) and consists of four units; two of each design in different fabric combinations. Refer to Accurate Seam Allowance on page 108. Whenever possible use Assembly Line Method on page 108. Press seams in direction of arrows.

## Making the Block

1. Refer to Quick Corner Triangles on page 108. Making quick corner triangle units, sew four 3" Fabric B squares to one 5½" Fabric A square as shown. Press. Make twelve and label Unit 1.

### Unit 1

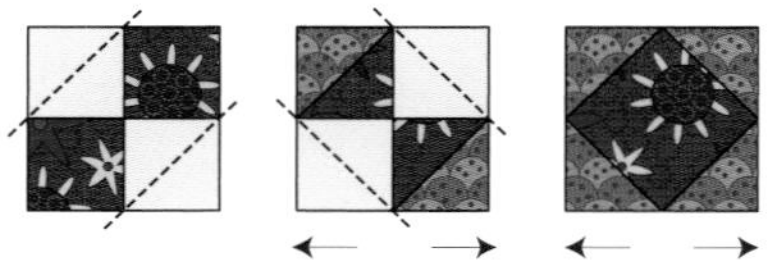

Fabric B = 3 x 3
Fabric A = 5½ x 5½
Make 12

2. Making quick corner triangle units, sew four 3" Fabric C squares to one 5½" Fabric A square as shown. Press. Make twelve and label Unit 2.

### Unit 2

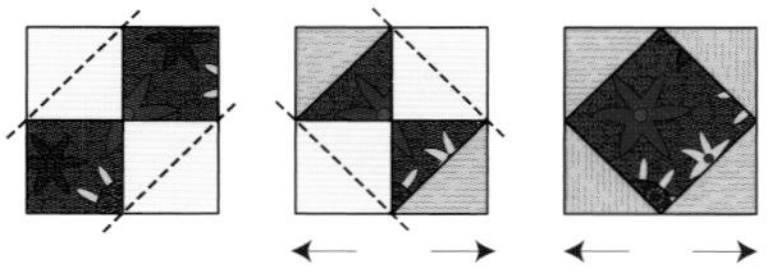

Fabric C = 3 x 3
Fabric A = 5½ x 5½
Make 12

| Sunny Side Up Lap Quilt Finished Size: 42" x 54" | FIRST CUT | | SECOND CUT | |
|---|---|---|---|---|
| | Number of Strips or Pieces | Dimensions | Number of Pieces | Dimensions |
| Fabric A<br>Unit 1 and 2 Center<br>⅔ yard | 4 | 5½" x 42" | 24 | 5½" squares |
| Fabric B<br>Unit 1 Corners<br>½ yard | 4 | 3" x 42" | 48 | 3" squares |
| Fabric C<br>Unit 2 Corners<br>½ yard | 4 | 3" x 42" | 48 | 3" squares |
| Fabric D<br>Unit 3 Light<br>⅜ yard | 3 | 3½" x 42" | 24 | 3½" squares |
| Fabric E<br>Unit 3 Dark<br>⅜ yard | 3 | 3½" x 42" | 24 | 3½" squares |
| Fabric F<br>Unit 4 Light<br>⅜ yard | 3 | 3½" x 42" | 24 | 3½" squares |
| Fabric G<br>Unit 4 Dark<br>⅜ yard | 3 | 3½" x 42" | 24 | 3½" squares |
| Sashing<br>1 yard | 19 | 1½" x 42" | 5<br>20<br>24 | 1½" x 35½"<br>1½" x 11½"<br>1½" x 5½" |
| Outside Border<br>½ yard | 5 | 2½" x 42" | | |
| Binding<br>½ yard<br>OR ¾ Bias | 5<br><br>1 | 2¾" x 42"<br>OR<br>26" square (Bias) | | |
| Backing - 2⅔ yards<br>Batting - 48" x 60" | | | | |

Two easy blocks are framed by a lattice to create a quilt with double diagonal interest and appeal. The striped fabric was the inspiration for this striking color combination. Drape the quilt on a bench for a splash of color and comfort.

## Sunny Side Up LAP QUILT
Finished Size: 42" x 54"

4. Sew two units from step 3 together as shown. Press. Make twenty-four. Sew two of these units together as shown. Refer to Twisting Seams on page 108. Press. Make twelve and label Unit 3.

**Unit 3**

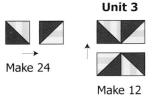

Make 24

Make 12

5. Draw a diagonal line on wrong side of one 3½" Fabric F square. Place marked square and one 3½" Fabric G square right sides together. Sew scant ¼" away from drawn line on both sides to make half-square triangles as shown. Make twenty-four. Cut on drawn line and press. Square to 3". This will make forty-eight half-square triangle units.

Fabric F = 3½ x 3½     Square to 3"
Fabric G = 3½ x 3½     Make 48
Make 24                Half-square Triangles

6. Sew two units from step 5 together as shown. Press. Make twenty-four. Sew two of these units together as shown. Twist seams. Press. Make twelve and label Unit 4.

**Unit 4**

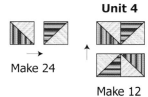

Make 24

Make 12

3. Draw a diagonal line on wrong side of one 3½" Fabric D square. Place marked square and one 3½" Fabric E square right sides together. Sew scant ¼" away from drawn line on both sides to make half-square triangles as shown. Make twenty-four. Cut on drawn line and press. Square to 3". This will make forty-eight half-square triangle units.

Fabric D = 3½ x 3½     Square to 3"
Fabric E = 3½ x 3½     Make 48
Make 24                Half-square Triangles

7. Sew one 1½" x 5½" Sashing strip between one Unit 1 and one Unit 3 as shown. Press. Make twelve.

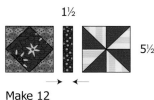

Make 12

8. Sew one 1½" x 5½" Sashing strip between one Unit 4 and one Unit 2 as shown. Press. Make twelve.

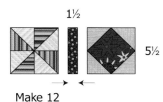

Make 12

9. Sew one 1½" x 11½" Sashing strip between one unit from step 1 and one unit from step 2 as shown. Press. Make twelve. Block measures 11½".

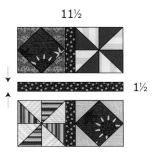

Make 12
Block measures 11½" square

## Assembling the Quilt

1. Arrange and sew together three blocks, and two 1½" x 11½" Sashing strips, as shown. Press. Make four.

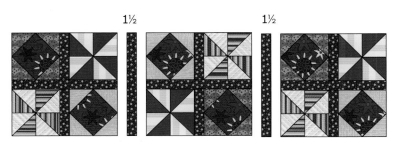

Make 4

2. Referring to photo on page 49 and layout on page 50, arrange and sew together five 1½" x 35½" Sashing strips and rows from step 1, rotating rows as necessary. Press seams toward Sashing strips.

## Adding the Borders

1. Refer to Adding the Borders on page 110. Sew 1½" x 42" Sashing strips end-to-end to make one continusous 1½"-wide Sashing strip. Measure quilt through center from top to bottom. Cut two 1½"-wide Sashing strips to this measurement. Sew to sides of quilt. Press.

2. Sew 2½" x 42" Outside Border strips together end-to-end to make one continuous 2½"-wide Outside Border strip. Measure quilt through center from side to side. Cut two 2½"-wide Outside Border strips to this measurement. Sew to top and bottom of quilt. Press seams toward border.

3. Measure quilt through center from top to bottom, including borders just added. Cut two 2½"-wide Outside Border strips to this measurement. Sew to sides of quilt. Press.

## Layering and Finishing

1. Cut backing crosswise into two equal pieces. Sew pieces together lengthwise to make one 48" x 80" (approximate) backing piece. Press and trim to 48" x 60".

2. Referring to Layering the Quilt on page 110, arrange and baste backing, batting, and top together. Hand or machine quilt as desired.

3. Refer to Making Bias Strips on page 110. Start with a 26" Binding square to cut bias strip. Approximately 200" of 2¾"-wide binding is needed. Refer to Binding the Quilt on page 110. Bind quilt to finish.

# Bodacious BANNER

| Bodacious Banner Finished Size: 25" x 29½" | FIRST CUT | | SECOND CUT | |
|---|---|---|---|---|
| | Number of Strips or Pieces | Dimensions | Number of Pieces | Dimensions |
| **Fabric A** Small Light Pinwheels Scrap *each of 4 Fabrics* | 2* | 3½" squares *cut for each fabric* | | |
| **Fabric B** Small Dark Pinwheels Scrap *each of 4 Fabrics* | 2* | 3½" squares *cut for each fabric* | | |
| **Fabric C** Large Light Pinwheels ¼ yard | 1 | 6" x 42" | 2 | 6" squares |
| **Fabric D** Large Dark Pinwheels ¼ yard | 1 | 6" x 42" | 2 | 6" squares |
| **First Border** ⅙ yard | 3 | 1" x 42" | 2 / 3 | 1" x 22" / 1" x 10½" |
| **Second Border** ⅛ yard | 2 | 1¼" x 42" | 2 / 2 | 1¼" x 23½" / 1¼" x 11½" |
| **Outside Border** ⅝ yard | 1 / 3 | 6¼" x 42" / 3¾" x 42" | 1 / 2 / 1 | 6¼" x 13" / 3¾" x 32½" / 3¾" x 13" |
| **Banner Backing** ⅝ yard | 1 | 19½" x 42" | 1 | 19½" x 32½" |
| **Accent Banner** 1½ yards | 2 | 25½" x 42" | 2 | 25½" x 25½" |
| Appliqués - Assorted Scraps Lightweight Fusible Web - ⅛ yard | | | | |

## Fabric Requirements and Cutting Instructions

Read all instructions before beginning and use ¼"-wide seam allowances throughout. Read Cutting Strips and Pieces on page 108 prior to cutting fabric.

## Getting Started

Pinwheel blocks in two sizes, 5½" and 10½" (unfinished), add depth and movement to this banner. The banner and a seperate accent piece are joined together to make a unique banner that will catch the breeze as you enjoy the outdoors. Refer to Accurate Seam Allowance on page 108. Whenever possible use Assembly Line Method on page 108. Press seams in direction of arrows.

## Making the Banner

1. Draw a diagonal line on wrong side of one 3½" Fabric A square. Place marked square and one 3½" Fabric B square right sides together. Sew scant ¼" away from drawn line on both sides to make half-square triangles as shown. Make two. Cut on drawn line and press. Square to 3". This will make four half-square triangle units.

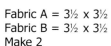

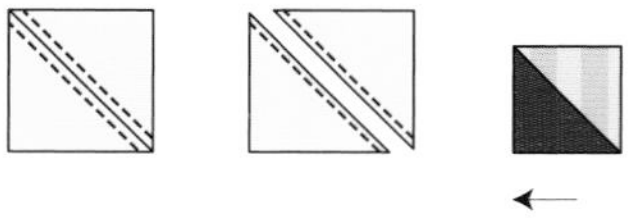

Fabric A = 3½ x 3½
Fabric B = 3½ x 3½
Make 2

Square to 3"
Make 4
Half-square Triangles

Declare the summer games open with this playful banner that adds pageantry and pizzazz to outdoor spaces. Hang the banner from a pole or beam for a welcoming entry to the garden. This pieced beauty is layered with a striped fabric for added interest.

**Bodacious BANNER**

Finished Size: 25" x 29½"

4. Sew two units from steps 2 and 3 together as shown. Press. Make two. Sew these units together. Twist seams. Press. Block measures 10½" square.

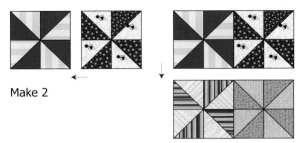

Make 2

Block measures 10½" square

5. Draw a diagonal line on wrong side of one 6" Fabric C square. Place marked square and one 6" Fabric D square right sides together. Sew scant ¼" away from drawn line on both sides to make half-square triangles as shown. Make two. Cut on drawn line and press. Square to 5½". This will make four half-square triangle units.

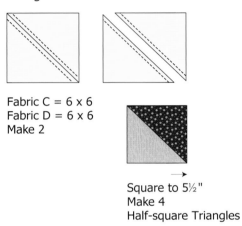

Fabric C = 6 x 6
Fabric D = 6 x 6
Make 2

Square to 5½"
Make 4
Half-square Triangles

2. Sew two units from step 1 together as shown. Press. Sew these units together. Refer to Twisting Seams on page 108. Press.

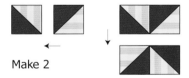

Make 2

3. Referring to steps 1 and 2 to make three different pinwheels using different combinations of Fabric A and B 3½" squares.

Make 3
(in different fabric combinations)

6. Sew two units from step 5 together as shown. Press. Make two. Sew these units together. Twist seams. Press. Block measures 10½" square.

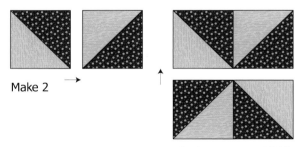

Make 2

Block measures 10½" square

7. Referring to photo on page 53 and layout, sew one 1" x 10½" First Border strip between blocks from steps 4 and 6. Press.

## Adding the Borders

1. Sew two 1" x 10½" First Border strips to top and bottom of banner. Press seams toward border. Sew two 1" x 22" First Border strips to sides of banner. Press.

2. Sew two 1¼" x 11½" Second Border strips to top and bottom of banner. Press seams toward border just sewn. Sew two 1¼" x 23½" Second Border strips to sides of banner. Press.

3. Sew one 6¼" x 13" Outside Border strip to top of banner and one 3¾" x 13" Outside Border strips to bottom of banner. Press seams toward borders just sewn. Sew two 3¾" x 32½" Outside Border strips to sides of banner. Press.

## Adding the Appliqués

Refer to appliqué instructions on page 109. Our instructions are for Quick-Fuse Appliqué, but if you prefer hand appliqué add ¼"-wide seam allowances.

1. Use patterns on pages 62 and 111 to trace ten flower petals, one 3" and one 2", one 1¾" and two 1" circles on paper side of fusible web. Use appropriate fabrics to prepare all appliqués for fusing.

2. Refer to photo on page 53 and layout on page 54 to position and fuse appliqués to quilt. Finish appliqué edges with machine satin stitch or other decorative stitching as desired.

## Finishing the Banner

1. Layer and center banner top and 19½" x 32½" backing piece right sides together. Using ¼"-wide seam, stitch around sides and bottom edge, leaving top edge open for turning. Clip corners, turn, and press. Baste top edge closed. Note: Raw edges are showing.

2. Place two 25½" Accent Banner pieces right sides together. Using ¼"-wide seam, stitch around sides and bottom edge, leaving top edge open for turning. Clip corners, turn, and press. Baste top edge closed. Note: Raw edges are showing.

3. Referring to photo on page 53 and layout on page 54, center banner top from step 1 on top of Accent Banner from step 2 aligning top raw edges. Pin layers together. Fold top edges under ¼" and press.

4. Fold top edges toward the back leaving 3¼" Outside Border showing along the banner's front top edge. Edge stitch along fold lines to make a rod pocket.

# Garden Patches
# TABLE QUILT

## Fabric Requirements and Cutting Instructions

Read all instructions before beginning and use ¼"-wide seam allowances throughout. Read Cutting Strips and Pieces on page 108 prior to cutting fabric.

## Getting Started

This colorful quilt will add fun to any outdoor setting. The quilt is made with an assortment of different colored fabric squares. Extra pieces are cut to allow for different placement options while laying out the quilt. Refer to Accurate Seam Allowance on page 108. Whenever possible use Assembly Line Method on page 108. Press seams in direction of arrows.

## Making the Quilt

To obtain a scrappy look to your quilt we recommend laying out all pieces prior to sewing quilt together. Refer to layout on page 58 and photo on page 57 for guidance. After quilt layout is as desired, continue with step instructions.

| Garden Patches Table Quilt Finished Size: 40" x 40" | FIRST CUT | | SECOND CUT | |
|---|---|---|---|---|
| | Number of Strips or Pieces | Dimensions | Number of Pieces | Dimensions |
| **Fabric A** Background ½ yard | 6 | 2½" x 42" | 60 | 2½" x 3½" |
| **Fabric B** Large & Small Squares ⅛ yard each of 8 Fabrics | 1* | 3½" x 42" *cut for each fabric | 4* 3* | 3½" squares 2½" squares |
| **Fabric C** Corner, Large & Small Squares ⅛ yard | 1 | 3½" x 42" | 3 5 | 3½" squares 2½" squares |
| **Fabric D** Corner, Large & Small Squares ⅛ yard | 1 | 3½" x 42" | 7 3 | 3½" squares 2½" squares |
| **First Border** ¼ yard | 4 | 1¼" x 42" | 2 2 | 1¼" x 30" 1¼" x 28½" |
| **Second, Fourth & Outside Border** ⅔ yard | 8 4 | 1¾" x 42" 1½" x 42" | 4 4 4 | 1¾" x 34" 1¾" x 30" 1½" x 34" |
| **Third Border** ¼ yard | 4 | 1¼" x 42" | 4 | 1¼" x 30" |
| **Fifth Border** ¼ yard | 4 | 1¼" x 42" | 4 | 1¼" x 34" |
| **Binding** ⅓ yard | 4 | 2¼" x 42" ¼" finished binding | | |

Backing - 1¼ yards (Fabric needs to be at least 44"-wide)
Batting - 44" x 44"

1. Sew one 3½" Fabric B square to one 2½" x 3½" Fabric A piece as shown. Press. Make thirty using an assortment of 3½" Fabric B, C, and D squares.

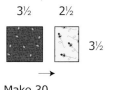

3½    2½

3½

Make 30
(using assorted Fabric B, C & D pieces)

Plant beautiful patches of color on your patio with an easy and inviting table quilt.
Multi-colored squares in two sizes create an organized table top that's highlighted with
an unusual and interesting border treatment.

2. Arrange and sew together five units from step 1 and one 3½" Fabric B, C, or D square as shown. Press. Make six rows.

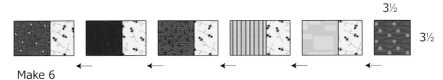

3½

3½

Make 6

3. Sew one 2½" x 3½" Fabric A piece to one 2½" Fabric B, C, or D square as shown. Press. Make twenty-five using an assortment of Fabric B, C, and D squares.

3½     2½

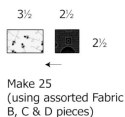

2½

Make 25
(using assorted Fabric
B, C & D pieces)

4. Arrange and sew together five units from step 3 and one 2½" x 3½" Fabric A piece as shown. Press. Make five rows.

3½

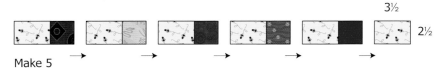

2½

Make 5

5. Referring to photo on page 57 and layout, arrange and sew rows from steps 2 and 4 together. Press.

## Adding the Borders

1. Sew two 1¼" x 28½" First Border strips to top and bottom of quilt. Press seams toward border. Sew 1¼" x 30" First Border strips to the sides. Press.

2. Sew one 1¾" x 30" Second Border strip to one 1¼" x 30" Third Border strip to make a strip set. Press seams toward Second Border. Make four. Sew two strip sets to top and bottom of quilt. Press.

### Garden Patches TABLE QUILT
Finished Size: 40" x 40"

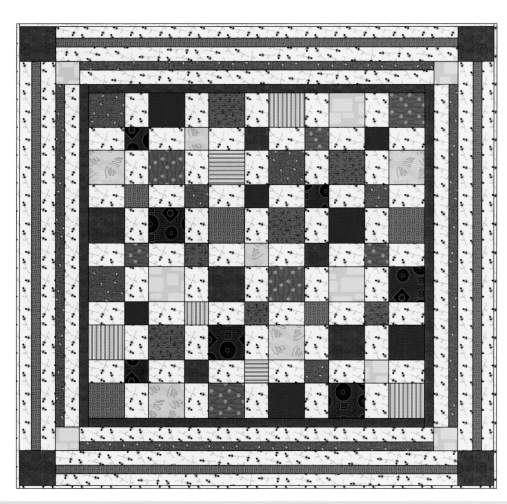

3. Sew one strip set from step 2 between two 2½" Fabric C squares. Press seams toward Fabric C. Make two. Sew these units to sides of quilt. Press.

4. Sew one 1¼" x 34" Fifth Border strip between one 1¾" x 34" Fourth Border strip and one 1½" x 34" Outside Border strip. Press seams toward center. Make four strip sets. Sew two strip sets to top and bottom of quilt noting position of Outside Border. Press.

5. Sew one strip set from step 4 between two 3½" Fabric D squares. Press seams toward Fabric D. Make two. Sew these units to sides of quilt. Press.

## Layering and Finishing

1. Referring to Layering the Quilt on page 110, arrange and baste backing, batting, and top together. Hand or machine quilt as desired.

2. Refer to Binding the Quilt on page 110. Use 2¼"-wide Binding strips to bind quilt. Note: Finished width of binding is ¼" instead of our normal ½".

# It's in the details

There's nothing formal about outdoor dining!

Create a casual centerpiece by putting sunflowers and black-eyed-susans in an old enameled bowl.

Invite the bees to the party with a metal and wire bee plucked from a flowerbox.

Enjoy napkins of many colors—there's no matchy-matchy at this party! Use left-over yardage from the table quilt to make two-sided 18" napkins in multiple color combinations. Roll the napkins into painted and distressed wooden napkin rings for even more of a color mix.

# Fashionable Flowers
## PILLOW

## Fabric Requirements and Cutting Instructions

Read all instructions before beginning and use ¼"-wide seam allowances throughout.

## Getting Started

This eye-catching pillow is fast and fun to make and a colorful accent for a garden chair.

## Making the Pillow

1. Sew one 8½" Center square between two 1¼" x 8½" First Border strips. Press seams toward border. Sew this unit between two 1¼" x 10" First Border strips. Press.

2. Sew one unit from step 1 between two 1½" x 10" Second Border strips. Press seams toward border. Sew this unit between two 1½" x 12" Second Border strips. Press.

3. Sew one unit from step 2 between two 1¾" x 12" Outside Border strips. Press seams toward border. Sew this unit between two 1¾" x 14½" Outside Border strips. Press.

## Adding the Appliqués

Refer to appliqué instructions on page 109. Our instructions are for Quick-Fuse Appliqué, but if you prefer hand appliqué add ¼"-wide seam allowances.

1. Use patterns on page 62 to trace flowers and flower centers on paper side of fusible web. Use appropriate fabrics to prepare all appliqués for fusing.

2. Refer to photo to position and fuse appliqués to pillow top. Finish appliqué edges with machine satin stitch or other decorative stitching as desired.

**Fashionable Flowers PILLOW**
Finished Size: 14" x 14"

## Finishing the Pillow

1. Refer to Finishing Pillows on page 110, step 1, to prepare pillow top for quilting. Quilt as desired.

2. Sew a button to each flower center.

3. Use two 10" x 14½" backing pieces and refer to Finishing Pillows, page 110, steps 2-4, to sew backing.

4. Insert 14" pillow form or refer to Pillow Forms page 111 to make a pillow form if desired

Flowers bloom everywhere in this garden! Stylized flowers decorate two pillows that are perfect to add delightful drama to garden furniture.

## Materials Needed

Center - ⅓ yard
    One 8½" square
First Border - ⅛ yard
    Two 1¼" x 10"
    Two 1¼" x 8½"
Second Border - ⅙ yard
    Two 1½" x 12"
    Two 1½" x 10"
Outside Border - ⅙ yard
    Two 1¾" x 14½"
    Two 1¾" x 12"
Flower Appliqués - Assorted scraps
Backing - Two 10" x 14½"
Batting and Lining - 16" x 16"
Lightweight Fusible Web - ⅓ yard
Assorted Buttons - 4
14" Pillow Form
    OR Optional Pillow Form - ½ yard
        Two 14½" Fabric Squares
        Polyester Fiberfill

Four festive flowers are accented with buttons and borders on a pillow that will add playful punch to a sun room or outdoor setting. The same appliqué shape is enlarged and embellished differently for the Dipsy Daisy Pillow. When combining appliquéd pillows in a setting, change the scale and dominant colors from one pillow to another so that pillows will both mix and match.

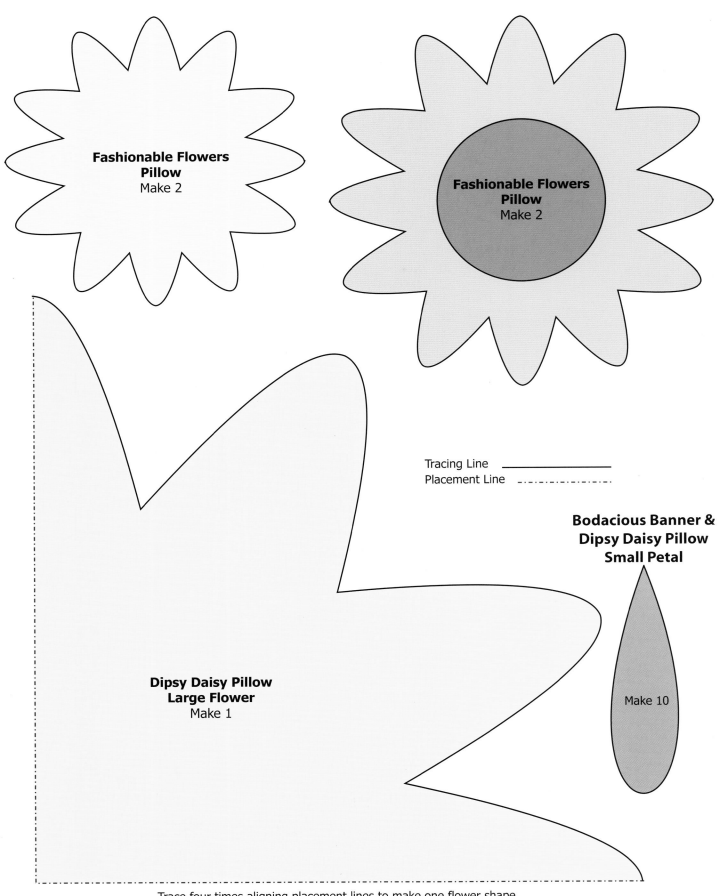

**Fashionable Flowers
Pillow**
Make 2

**Fashionable Flowers
Pillow**
Make 2

Tracing Line
Placement Line

**Bodacious Banner &
Dipsy Daisy Pillow
Small Petal**

Make 10

**Dipsy Daisy Pillow
Large Flower**
Make 1

Trace four times aligning placement lines to make one flower shape.

# Dipsy Daisy PILLOW

**Make a bold statement with this fun-loving pillow.**

## Materials Needed

Background and Backing - ⅞ yard
 One 16½" square
 Two 11" x 16½"
Large Flower Appliqués - Fat Quarter
Small Petal Appliqués - Scrap
Circle Appliqués - Assorted scraps
Lining - 20" x 20"
Batting - 20" x 20"
Lightweight Fusible Web - ⅞ yard
16" Pillow Form
 OR Optional Pillow Form - ½ yard
 Two 16½" Fabric Squares
 Polyester Fiberfill

## Fabric Requirements and Cutting Instructions

Read all instructions before beginning and use ¼"-wide seam allowances throughout. Read Cutting Strips and Pieces on page 108 prior to cutting fabric.

## Getting Started

This easy to make applique pillow is a great accent to any of our Outdoor Room projects.

## Adding the Appliqués

Refer to appliqué instructions on page 109. Our instructions are for Quick-Fuse Appliqué, but if you prefer hand appliqué add ¼"-wide seam allowances.

1. Use patterns on pages 62 and 111 to trace Large Flower, Small Petals, and 5½", 3½", and 2" circles on paper side of fusible web. Use appropriate fabrics to prepare all appliqués for fusing.

2. Refer to photo to position and fuse appliqués to 16½" Background square. Finish appliqué edges with machine satin stitch or other decorative stitching as desired.

## Finishing the Pillow

1. Refer to Finishing Pillows on page 111, step 1, to prepare pillow top for quilting. Quilt as desired.

2. Use two 11" x 16½" backing pieces and refer to Finishing Pillows, page 111, steps 2-4, to sew backing.

3. Insert 16" pillow form or refer to Pillow Forms page 111 to make a pillow form if desired.

**Dipsy Daisy PILLOW**
Finished Size: 16" x 16"

# Pots with PIZZAZZ

## Preparing the Flowerpots

Paint outside and at least 4" of inside of each flowerpot with Gesso. Allow to dry thoroughly. Lightly sand flowerpots.

## Painting the Daisy Flowerpot

1. Trace one of each petal shape on page 65 onto paper. Trace a 2" circle and 3" circle on page 111 onto paper. Use double-stick tape to hold patterns onto Magic Sponge. Using small sharp scissors, cut out each shape from Magic Sponge. Dampen sponge shapes with water to expand.

2. Paint rim of pot with Light Buttermilk. Paint body of the pot with Hauser Light Green. Two or more coats may be needed for good coverage. Allow paint to dry thoroughly after each coat.

3. Determine placement of large and small daisies and mark circle centers with pencil. Pour a small amount of Burnt Umber paint onto plate or palette. Rub slightly damp large circle sponge into paint until sponge is covered. Carefully place circle on flowerpot rim and gently and evenly pat sponge to transfer paint onto the flowerpot. Repeat this process for additional large flower centers then repeat process to add small flower centers.

4. Pour a small amount of Golden Straw paint on a clean palette or plate. Repeat processes from step 3 to add petals around each sunflower center. Allow to dry.

5. Using a small paintbrush, lightly outline each petal with Burnt Umber paint. Allow to dry.

6. Apply Antiquing Gel to entire pot, following manufacturer's directions. When dry, apply several coats of exterior varnish, following manufacturer's directions.

## Materials Needed

**Daisy Flowerpot:** 14½" high and 12" diameter or similar

**Stripe Flowerpot:** 9½" high and 10½" diameter or similar

Gesso

Fine Sandpaper

Assorted Paintbrushes

Sea Sponge

Small Sharp Scissors

Double-stick Tape

Paper Plate or Paper Palette

Delta Ceramcoat® Acrylic Paints Tompte Red and Burnt Umber

Americana® Acrylic Paints Hauser Light Green, Golden Straw, Cocoa, Light Buttermilk

Delta Texture Magic™ Antiquing Gel

Exterior Varnish

Magic Sponge™*

*Magic Sponge™ is thinly compressed cellulose that expands when wet. It is available at many art and craft supply stores.

## Painting the Striped Pot

1. Basecoat rim of flowerpot with Golden Straw paint and basecoat bottom of pot with Burnt Umber. Two or more coats of paint may be needed for good coverage. Allow paint to dry thoroughly between each coat.

2. Dampen sea sponge with water, wring well, then dip in both burnt umber and cocoa paint. Blot sponge on paper towel, then sponge color onto bottom of pot using a tapping motion. Sponge lightly for a mottled effect. Allow to dry.

3. Using a pencil, draw stripes onto painted rim of flowerpot. Using a paintbrush the width of desired stripe, hand-paint stripes, applying one color at a time (Tompte Red, Cocoa and Hauser Light Green.) Allow paint to dry between colors. Two or more coats of paint may be needed for good coverage.

4. When flowerpot is thoroughly dry, apply exterior varnish following manufacturer's directions.

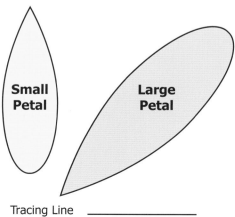

**Small Petal**

**Large Petal**

Tracing Line _____

Paint your flowerpots to match other outdoor room furnishings with simple sponge-stamping and painting techniques.

# Bee Happy DOOR BANNER

## Getting Started

Layers of fabrics are quick-fused together and then accented with bee appliqués. We finished the sections using hand embroidery stitches (big stitch, blanket stitch, and stem stitch), but this can easily be done by machine if desired.

## Making the Banner

1. Following manufacturer's instructions, fuse lightweight fusible web to back of the following pieces, 8" x 12½" Fabric A piece, 9" x 14½" Fabric B piece, ½" x 9" and ½" x 5" Fabric C strips.

2. Refer to diagram below to measure and mark Fabric A top corners 1½" in toward center and 3" down sides as shown. Draw a line connecting these marks. Cut on drawn lines.

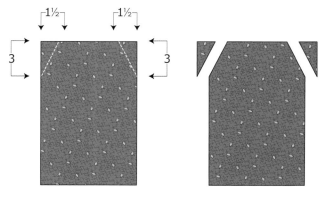

3. Center and fuse Fabric A piece to Fabric B piece. (Note: Top and bottom edges will have more of Fabric B showing than side edges.) Measure, mark, and cut Fabric B angle, matching the side edge distance, noted with arrows on diagram.

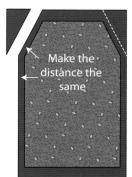

Make the distance the same

4. Refer to appliqué instructions on page 109. Our instructions are for Quick-Fuse Appliqué, but if you prefer hand appliqué, reverse patterns and add ¼"-wide seam allowances. Use patterns on page 67 to trace bees on paper side of fusible web. Use appropriate fabrics to prepare all appliqués for fusing.

Don't worry, bee happy! Welcome friends to the garden with this whimsical bee banner. Made of wool and cotton and embellished with hand-stitching and buttons, this banner is a fun rainy-day project.

5. Refer to photo to position and fuse appliqués to quilt.

6. Referring to photo, fuse ½" x 5" to top edge of banner and ½" x 9" Fabric C pieces to bottom edge. Trim top edge to match banner angle edges.

7. Refer to photo and Embroidery Stitch Guide on page 111. Using a stem stitch and three strands of embroidery floss, stitch bees' antennas. Using a straight stitch, add a centerline to each wing. Using a blanket stitch and three strands of embroidery floss, stitch around bees' head and body. Using a temporary fabric marker, measure and draw a line ¾" from top Fabric A edge and ½" from angle, side and bottom edges. Using a running stitch and three strands of embroidery floss stitch along marked line.

8. Cut, center and fuse 9" x 14½" backing piece to unit from step 7, wrong sides together. Trim backing to match front. Using a blanket stitch and three strands of embroidery floss, stitch banner and backing together around all edges.

9. Referring to photo, sew two matching buttons to bottom of banner and seven assorted buttons to top of banner.

## Materials Needed

Fabric A (Appliqué Background) - ⅓ yard
    One 8" x 12½"

Fabric B (Background) - ⅓ yard wool
    One 9" x 14½"

Fabric C (Accent) - ⅛ yard wool
    One ½" x 9"
    One ½" x 5"

Appliqués - Assorted scraps

Backing - ⅓ yard

Lightweight Fusible Web - ½ yard

Embroidery Floss - Gold, Blue, Black and Tan

Buttons - 9 Assorted

## Bee Happy Door Banner

Pattern is reversed for use
with Quick-Fuse Applique (page 109)

Tracing Line _____
Tracing Line - - - - - - - - - - - -
(will be hidden behind other fabrics)
Embroidery Placement · · · · · · · · · · ·
Straight Stitch _____

## Bee Happy DOOR BANNER

Finished Size: 9" x 14"

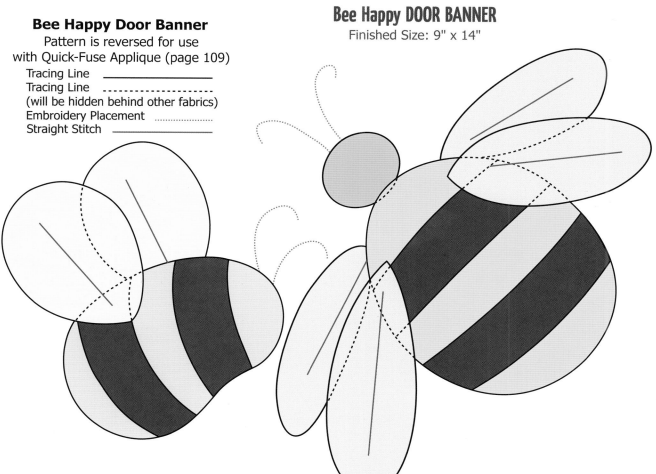

# Glowing Glass
# LANTERN

## Making the Lantern

Straight pieces of glass in a variety of colors and sizes are used for this project. Using photo as a guide, cut glass pieces into widths ranging from ⅜ " – ⅝ " and a variety of lengths. Usable area on the lantern shown is 6", so lengths were cut ranging from 1½" to 5".

## Cutting Glass

1. Cover a flat work surface with several layers of newspaper. Hold cutter in a comfortable position. It is important to lubricate the cutter's wheel each time before scoring glass.

2. You must wear Safety Glasses while working with glass. Always stand when cutting glass to obtain proper pressure while cutting. Glass is not cut, but scored, which doesn't take a lot of strength. Exerting comfortable pressure, the wheel of the cutter scratches the glass, creating a stress point. When pressure is applied to score line, glass should break along the line. When cutting stained glass, always score glass on its smoothest side.

3. Hold glass securely with one gloved hand while scoring with the other. Begin to score at the edge of the glass. Maintain an even pressure while scoring. Score line should be visible and a gentle 'ripping' sound should be heard. A heavy, white, fuzzy line indicates that too much pressure is being used.

4. Once the glass is scored, hold glass securely with one hand and position the jaws of the running pliers on score line. Press pliers on scored line and glass will break. There are several types of cutters and pliers, so be sure to follow specific instructions for your equipment. Practice this technique several times on clear glass before cutting stained glass.

5. Once glass is cut, arrange and glue glass pieces and gems on glass cylinder using clear adhesive caulk. If gems slide, use tape to hold gems in place until adhesive dries.

Edges of glass will be sharp, so handle lantern with care.

## Materials Needed

Purchased Outdoor Lantern with Metal Trim*

Transparent Glass in Assorted Colors**

Glass Gems in Assorted Colors and Sizes

Small Tube of Clear Adhesive Caulk

Glass Cutter, Lubricating Oil, and Running Pliers

Safety Goggles and Gloves

* Any size of glass lantern or a circular glass vase will work for this project.
**Some stained glass shops will sell scraps of glass. Transparent (Cathedral) glass is recommended for this project. Edges are sharp when cut. Keep out of reach of children.

Whether lit by a candle at night or glowing with sunlight during the day, this glass-embellished lantern will become one of your favorite outdoor room accessories. This simple technique is a great introduction to working with glass or try your hand at one of our other no-sharp-edges lantern projects.

## Make it Even Easier

If cutting glass is daunting, try one of these easy methods for outdoor lanterns.

1. Using adhesive caulk, adhere glass gems in a pattern or design to a clear glass vase. Do one side at a time to keep gems from slipping. Insert a candle and enjoy the glow.

2. String a variety of beads on stretchy cord and slide onto a recycled glass light cover or vase. Add a votive candle or tea light.

Unwind in a serene retreat filled with soft colors, comfortable pillows, soothing quilts, and nature-inspired accessories.

# Relaxation
# ROOMS

# Quiet Respite QUILT

| Quiet Respite Quilt<br>Finished Size: 63" x 83"<br>Queen Size Quilt:<br>83" x 103" | FIRST CUT | | SECOND CUT | |
|---|---|---|---|---|
| | Number of Strips or Pieces | Dimensions | Number of Pieces | Dimensions |
| **Fabric A**<br>Squares, Rectangles<br>& Outside Border<br>⅝ yard<br>⅞ yard<br>each of 9 Fabrics | 2*<br><br><br>2*<br>3*<br><br><br><br>3* | 6½" x 42"<br>*cut for each fabric<br><br>2½" x 42"<br>6½" x 42"<br>*cut for each fabric<br><br><br>2½" x 42" | 4*<br>6*<br>3*<br><br><br>7*<br>12*<br>5* | 6½" squares<br>6½" x 2½"<br>2½" squares<br><br><br>6½" squares<br>6½" x 2½"<br>2½" squares |
| **Fabric B**<br>Squares, Rectangles,<br>Outside Corners &<br>Border<br>⅝ yard<br>⅞ yard | 2<br><br><br>2<br>3<br><br><br>3 | 6½" x 42"<br><br><br>2½" x 42"<br>6½" x 42"<br><br><br>2½" x 42" | 8<br>6<br>3<br><br>10<br>12<br>5 | 6½" squares<br>6½" x 2½"<br>2½" squares<br><br>6½" squares<br>6½" x 2½"<br>2½" squares |
| **Fabric C**<br>Sashing, First &<br>Outside Borders<br>2 yards<br>3⅛ yards | 10<br>27<br><br>13<br>51 | 2½" x 42"<br>1½" x 42"<br><br>2½" x 42"<br>1½" x 42" | 56<br>48<br><br>108<br>96 | 1½" x 6½"<br>1½" x 2½"<br><br>1½" x 6½"<br>1½" x 2½" |
| **Binding**<br>¾ yard<br>1 yard | 8<br>11 | 2¾" x 42"<br>2¾" x 42" | | |
| Backing - 5 yards<br>Batting - 70" x 90"<br>Backing - 7½ yards<br>Batting - 90" x 110" | | | | |

## Fabric Requirements and Cutting Instructions

Read all instructions before beginning and use ¼"-wide seam allowances throughout. Read Cutting Strips and Pieces on page 108 prior to cutting fabric. Note: Cutting chart lists Twin Size Quilt requirements in black and Queen Size in green.

## Getting Started

You will be able to cuddle up and relax in no time after making this easy and quick quilt. Refer to Accurate Seam Allowance on page 108. Whenever possible use Assembly Line Method on page 108. Press seams in direction of arrows.

## Making the Quilt

1. Sew one 6½" x 2½" Fabric A piece between two 1½" x 6½" Fabric C pieces as shown. Press. Make twenty-eight using assorted Fabric A and B pieces. Make fifty-four for Queen Size.

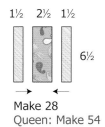

1½   2½   1½

6½

Make 28
Queen: Make 54

2. Sew one 2½" Fabric A square between two 1½" x 2½" Fabric C pieces as shown. Press. Make twenty-four using assorted Fabric A and B squares. Make forty-eight for Queen Size.

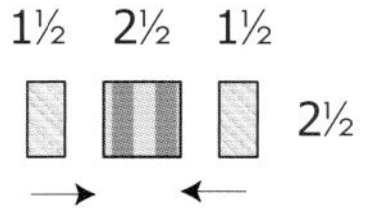

1½   2½   1½

2½

Make 24
Queen: Make 48

Relax your eyes and comfort your soul with a beautiful quilt featuring calming colors and orderly construction. Make the quilt in either twin or queen size with our easy instructions.

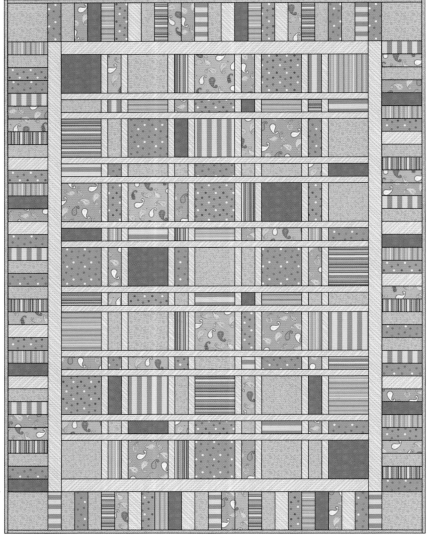

## Quiet Respite QUILT
Finished Size: 63" x 83"

5. Sew 1½" x 42" Fabric C strips together end-to-end to make one continuous 1½"-wide Fabric C strip. Press. Measure quilt through center from side to side. Cut twelve 1½"-wide Fabric C strips to this measurement. Queen Size: Cut sixteen strips.

6. Referring to photo on page 73 and layout, (Queen layout on page 75) arrange and sew rows and strips from steps 3-5 together. Press.

## Adding the Borders

1. Refer to Adding the Borders on page 110. Sew six 2½" x 42" Fabric C strips together end-to-end to make one continuous 2½"-wide Fabric C strip. Queen Size: Sew eight 2½" x 42" Fabric C strips together. Measure quilt through center from side to side. Cut two 2½"-wide Fabric C strips to this measurement. Sew to top and bottom of quilt. Press seams toward border.

2. Measure quilt through center from top to bottom including borders just added. Cut two 2½"-wide Fabric C strips to this measurement. Sew to sides of quilt. Press.

3. Arrange and sew together five 6½" assorted Fabric A and B squares and four assorted units from step 1 as shown. Press. Make seven. Queen Size: Sew together seven assorted Fabric A and B squares and six assorted units from step 1. Press. Make nine.

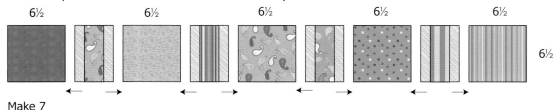

Make 7
Queen: Make 9

4. Arrange and sew together five 6½" x 2½" assorted Fabric A and B pieces and four assorted units from step 2 as shown. Press. Make six. Queen Size: Sew together seven 6½" x 2½" assorted Fabric A and B pieces and six assorted units from step 2. Press. Make eight.

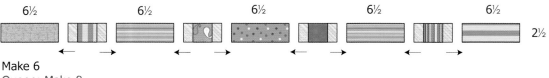

Make 6
Queen: Make 8

3. Strip sets are made using a variety of fabrics. Use four 2½" x 42" Fabric C strips and two of each 2½" x 42" Fabric A and B strips for a total of twenty-four strips. Arrange and sew together lengthwise six 2½" x 42" strips to make a strip set as shown. Press seams in one direction. Make four using different fabric combinations. Cut strip set into twenty-four 6½"-wide segments, six of each combination. Queen Size: Make five strip sets and cut a total of twenty-eight 6½" segments.

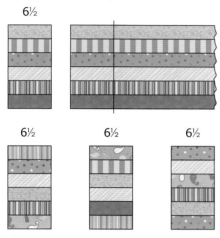

6½

6½          6½          6½

Make 4 strip sets
(in different combinations)
Cut a total of 24 segments
(6 of each combination)
Queen: Make 5 strip sets
Cut a total of 28 segments

4. Sew segments from step 3 together to make one long strip. Press. Extra pieces are included in strip to allow for fabric selection. Note: Do not use Fabric B or C next to corner squares.

5. Separate strip from step 4 by removing stitches to make two 25-pieced segments for top and bottom border strips and two 35-pieced segments for side borders strips. Queen Size: Make two 35-pieced segments and two 45-pieced segments.

6. Sew two 25-pieced segment strips to top and bottom of quilt. Press seams toward Fabric C border. Queen Size: Sew two 35-pieced segments to quilt.

7. Sew one 35-pieced segment strip between two 6½" Fabric B squares. Press seams toward Fabric C. Make two. Sew to sides of quilt. Press. Queen Size: Make two using 45-pieced segments and 6½" Fabric B squares.

## Layering and Finishing

1. Cut backing crosswise into two equal pieces. Sew pieces together lengthwise to make one 80" x 90" (approximate) backing piece. Queen Size: Cut backing crosswise into three equal pieces. Sew together to make one 90" x 120" (approximate) backing piece.

2. Referring to Layering the Quilt on page 110, arrange and baste backing, batting, and top together. Hand or machine quilt as desired.

3. Refer to Binding the Quilt on page 110. Sew 2¾" x 42" binding strips end-to-end to make one continuous 2¾"-wide binding strip. Bind quilt to finish.

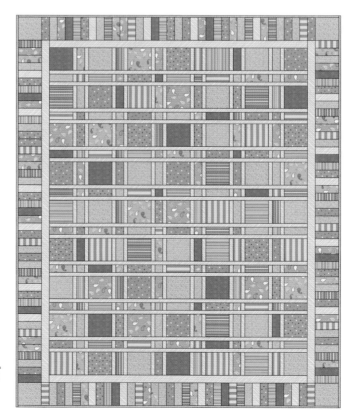

**Quiet Respite QUEEN SIZE QUILT**
Finished Size: 83" x 103"

# Paisley PILLOW SHAMS

Repetition of elements creates an air of serenity and relaxation. These pillow shams feature beautiful quilting on a creamy background and alternating borders on a series of shams.

## Materials Needed
### FOR ONE PILLOW

Fabric A (Center) - ⅜ yard
    One 11½" x 17½"
Fabric B (First Border) - ⅛ yard
    Two 2" x 17½"
    Two 2" x 14½"
Fabric C (Outside Border) - ½ yard
    Four 3½" x 20½"
Backing - ⅞ yard
    Two 26½" x 13"
Standard Pillow

## Fabric Requirements and Cutting Instructions

Read all instructions before beginning and use ¼"-wide seam allowances throughout. Read Cutting Strips and Pieces on page 108 prior to cutting fabric.

## Getting Started

Accent your bed with pillow shams. We used two different fabric combinations to add interest to the bed. Instructions given are for one pillow. Refer to Accurate Seam Allowance on page 108.

## Making Pillow Sham

1. Sew 11½" x 17½" Fabric A piece between two 2" x 17½" Fabric B strips. Press seams toward Fabric B. Sew this unit between two 2" x 14½" Fabric B strips. Press.

2. Sew unit from step 1 between two 3½" x 20½" Fabric C strips. Press seams toward Fabric C. Sew this unit between two 3½" x 20½" Fabric C strips. Press.

3. Refer to Finishing Pillows on page 111, step 1, to prepare pillow top for quilting. Quilt as desired.

4. Use two 26½" x 13" backing pieces and refer to Finishing Pillows, page 111, steps 2-4, to sew backing. Insert a standard bed pillow.

### Paisley PILLOW SHAMS
Finished Size:
20" x 26"

# It's in the details

Colors such as blue, purple, and green create a calm environment and foster feelings of peace and tranquility.

Candles provide soft light and fragrance in a relaxation room. Layering round and square shapes and glass and ceramic materials creates interest and novelty in this arrangement.

Plants refresh a room with the colors and shapes of the natural environment. A tabletop fountain can provide soothing sound and a water element in a room meant for relaxation.

Texture is an important way to add dimension in a room that uses lots of fabric. Baskets, rattan, wicker, and other woven surfaces add depth and visual interest.

What's more relaxing than a display of found objects from a walk on the beach? Here rocks, shells, coral, and sea glass are grouped in a weathered metal dish. As both reminders of happy times as well as soothing art objects with their soft water-washed colors and contours, these seaside souvenirs are the essence of relaxation.

# Restful Garden WALL ART

| Restful Garden Wall Art Finished Size: 30" x 22" | FIRST CUT | |
| --- | --- | --- |
| | Number of Strips or Pieces | Dimensions |
| Appliqué Background and Curved Border ⅓ yard wool each of 6 Fabrics | 1* | 9" square *cut for each fabric |
| Outside Border ⅞ yard | 2 2 | 3" x 25" 3" x 21" |
| Binding ⅜ yard | 4 | 2¾" x 42" |
| Backing - ¾ yard Batting - 34" x 26" Appliqués - Assorted wool and cotton scraps Lightweight Fusible Web - ¾ yard Iron-On Interfacing - 1 yard Embroidery Floss Assorted Beads Template Plastic or Pattern Paper | | |

## Fabric Requirements and Cutting Instructions

Read all instructions before beginning and use ½"-wide seam allowances throughout unless otherwise noted. Read Cutting Strips and Pieces on page 108 prior to cutting fabric.

## Getting Started

Stylized flowers, beads, and embroidery stitches enhance this wool wall quilt. Refer to Tips for Felting Wool on page 111 to prepare wool before cutting. Refer to Accurate Seam Allowance on page 108. Whenever possible use Assembly Line Method on page 108. Press seams in direction of arrows.

## Preparing the Pieces

1. Refer to page 80 to trace Curved Border pattern on template plastic or pattern paper. Using pattern, mark and cut ten border pieces from assorted wool scraps. Cut ten patterns from Outside Border fabric. This will be the backing for the Curved Border pieces.

2. Referring to manufacturer's instructions, apply interfacing to wrong side of 9" wool squares and Curved Border pieces.

## Adding the Appliqués

Refer to appliqué instructions on page 109. Our instructions are for Quick-Fuse Appliqué, but if you prefer hand appliqué, reverse patterns and add ¼"-wide seam allowances to cotton fabrics.

1. Use patterns on pages 80-83 to trace flowers on paper side of fusible web. Use appropriate fabrics to prepare all appliqués for fusing.

2. Refer to photo to position and fuse appliqués to 9" Appliqué Background squares. Finish appliqué edges with machine satin stitch or other decorative stitching as desired.

3. Refer to photo and Block patterns on pages 80-83 for embroidery stitch placements. Referring to Embroidery Stitch Guide on page 111, use three-strands of embroidery floss and using a straight stitch or stem stitch to add details to each flower. Embellish with beads as desired.

## Making the Wall Quilt

1. Referring to photo on page 79, and using ½"-wide seam allowance, arrange and sew together two rows with three blocks each. Press seams open. Sew rows together. Press.

2. Place one wool Curved Border piece with one backing piece right-sides-together. Using a ¼"-wide seam allowance, sew curved edge only, leaving straight edge free of stitching for turning. Clip curve. Turn right side out and press. Make ten Curved Border units.

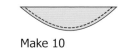

Make 10

Taking its inspiration from nature, this wool wall quilt features fantastical flowers embellished with stitchery and beads. Appliquéd squares are rounded off with comforting curves for a unique finish.

3. Arrange and baste three Curved Border units along top edge of quilt matching raw edges as shown. Repeat to arrange and baste three Curved Border units to bottom and two Curved Border units to each side of quilt. Keep Curved Border units in this position, curved edges towards center, while sewing Outside Border strips.

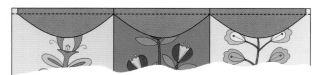

4. Using ½"-wide seam allowance, sew two 3" x 25" Outside Border strips to top and bottom of quilt. Press seams open. Sew 3" x 21" Outside Border strips to sides. Press.

## Layering and Finishing

1. Referring to Layering the Quilt on page 110, arrange and baste backing, batting, and top together. Hand or machine quilt as desired.

2. Refer to Binding the Quilt on page 110. Use 2¾"-wide Binding strips and ¼"-wide seam allowance to bind quilt.

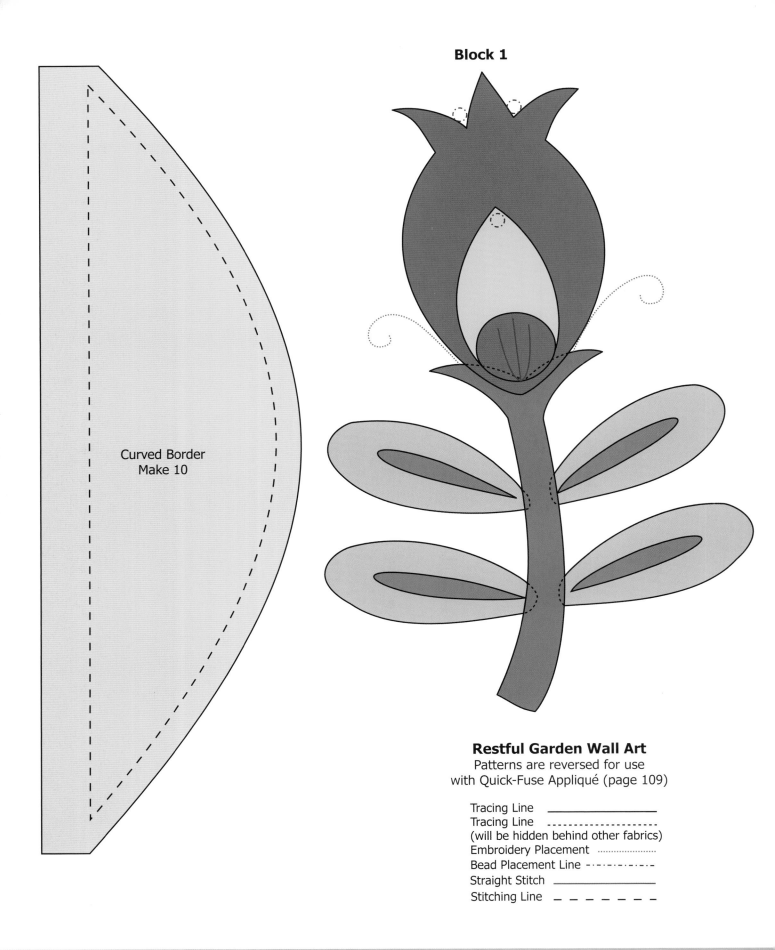

## Block 1

### Curved Border
Make 10

## Restful Garden Wall Art
Patterns are reversed for use
with Quick-Fuse Appliqué (page 109)

| | |
|---|---|
| Tracing Line | ——————— |
| Tracing Line | - - - - - - - - - - - |
| (will be hidden behind other fabrics) | |
| Embroidery Placement | ·················· |
| Bead Placement Line | -·—·—·—·—·— |
| Straight Stitch | ——————— |
| Stitching Line | – – – – – – – |

**Block 6**

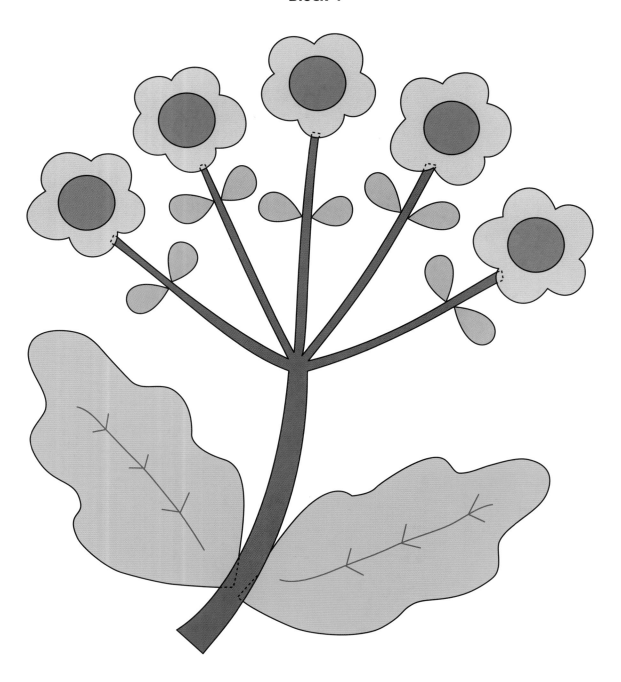

**Block 5**

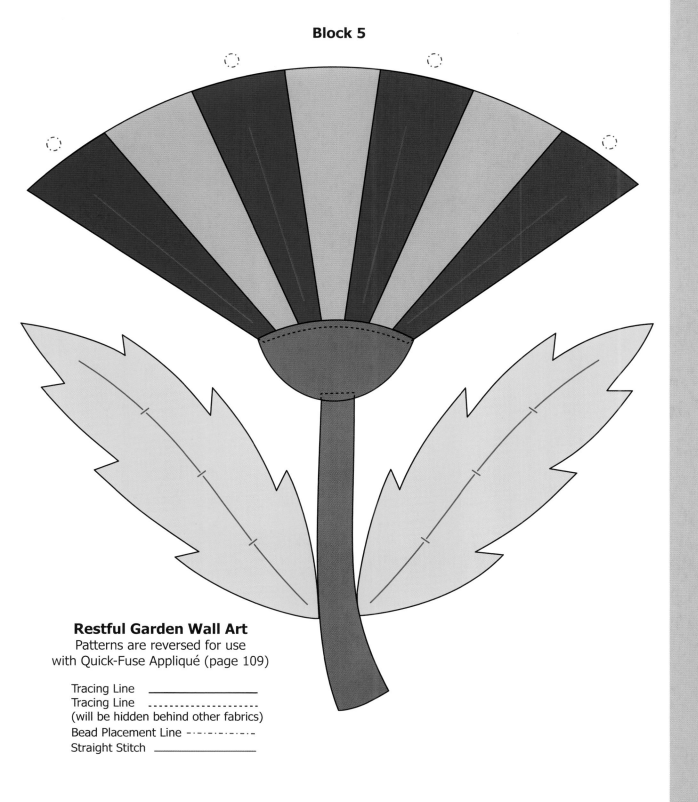

**Restful Garden Wall Art**
Patterns are reversed for use
with Quick-Fuse Appliqué (page 109)

Tracing Line _____
Tracing Line - - - - - - - - - - - - - - - - - -
(will be hidden behind other fabrics)
Bead Placement Line - - - · - - · - - · - - ·
Straight Stitch _____

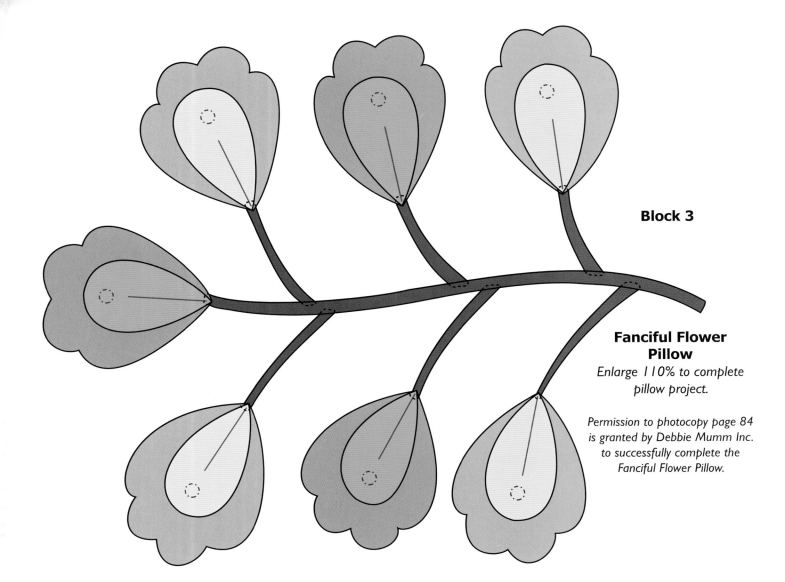

**Block 3**

**Fanciful Flower Pillow**

*Enlarge 110% to complete pillow project.*

*Permission to photocopy page 84 is granted by Debbie Mumm Inc. to successfully complete the Fanciful Flower Pillow.*

# Fanciful Flowers PILLOW

## Making the Pillow

Use Block 3 appliqué pattern to make a matching throw pillow.

1. Refer to Quick-Fuse Appliqué instructions on page 109. Enlarge appliqué pattern above by 110%. Trace flower on paper side of fusible web. Use appropriate fabrics to prepare all appliqués for fusing. Refer to photo to position and fuse appliqués to 11½" Appliqué Background square. Finish appliqué edges with machine satin stitch or other decorative stitching as desired.

## Materials Needed

Appliqué Background - ⅜ yard
  One 11½" square

Mock Piping - ⅛ yard
  Four 1" x 11½" pieces

Outside Border - ⅙ yard
  Two 2" x 14½" pieces
  Two 2" x 11½" pieces

Backing - ⅓ yard
  Two 10" x 14½" pieces

Appliqué - Assorted scraps

Lightweight Fusible Web - ¼ yard

14" Pillow Form

Assorted Buttons - 6

**Block 2**

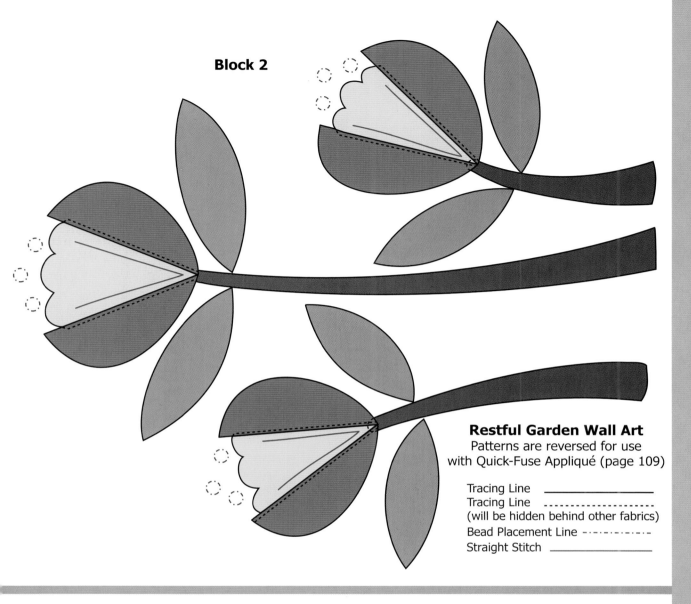

**Restful Garden Wall Art**
Patterns are reversed for use
with Quick-Fuse Appliqué (page 109)

Tracing Line _____
Tracing Line - - - - - - - - - - - - - - - - -
(will be hidden behind other fabrics)
Bead Placement Line - - · - - · - - · - -
Straight Stitch _____

2. Fold 1" x 11½" Mock Piping in half lengthwise wrong sides together to make a ½" x 11½" folded piece. Press. Make four.

3. Matching raw edges, layer two folded strips from step 2 on top and bottom of appliqué unit. Baste in place. Baste remaining folded strips to sides of unit.

4. Sew two 2" x 11½" Outside Border strips to top and bottom of unit from step 3. Press. Sew two 2" x 14½" Outside Border strips to sides. Press.

5. Refer to Finishing Pillows on page 111, step 1, to prepare pillow top for quilting. Quilt as desired.

6. Use two 10" x 14½" backing pieces and refer to Finishing Pillows, page 111, steps 2-4, to sew backing.

7. Insert 14" pillow form or refer to Pillow Forms on page 111 to make a pillow form if desired.

## Fanciful Flowers PILLOW
Finished Size: 14" x 14"

# Delightful Diagonal THROW

## Fabric Requirements and Cutting Instructions

Read all instructions before beginning and use ¼"-wide seam allowances throughout. Read Cutting Strips and Pieces on page 108 prior to cutting fabric.

## Getting Started

Diagonal stripes in various colors and different scales make a dazzling accent for our day bed. Refer to Accurate Seam Allowance on page 108. Whenever possible use Assembly Line Method on page 108. Press seams in direction of arrows.

## Cutting the Fabric

Referring to cutting chart, cut Fabric A First Cut strips, then cut lengths listed in Second Cuts column that are less than 40"-wide. Sew remaining strips end-to-end to make one continuous fabric strip for each width measurement. Press. Cut pieces wider than 40" from these strips. Label each strip's length for easy reference. Repeat for all fabrics.

## Making the Quilt

1. Fold each fabric strip in half to find center. Place a pin at this mark or press.

2. Align centerlines of strips and refer to diagram below. Sew one strip each of the following: 3" x 8", 2½" x 18", 2" x 29", 2½" x 35", 1½" x 44", 2" x 52", and 1½" x 60" Fabric A strips; 1½" x 10", 1½" x 41", and 1½" x 61" Fabric B strips; 2" x 30" and 3" x 57" Fabric C strips; 3" x 39" Fabric D strip; 5½" x 24" Fabric E strip; and 3½" x 49" Fabric F strip. Press seams in one direction. This completes the Top Section.

| Delightful Diagonal Throw Finished Size: 48" x 65" | FIRST CUT | | SECOND CUT | |
|---|---|---|---|---|
| | Number of Strips or Pieces | Dimensions | Number of Pieces | Dimensions |
| **Fabric A** 1⅛ yards | 4 | 3" x 42" | 1 | 3" x 62" |
| | | | 1 | 3" x 60" |
| | | | 2 | 3" x 8" |
| | 3 | 2½" x 42" | 1 | 2½" x 42" |
| | | | 1 | 2½" x 35" |
| | | | 1 | 2½" x 18" |
| | | | 1 | 2½" x 14" |
| | 4 | 2" x 42" | 1 | 2" x 52" |
| | | | 1 | 2" x 47" |
| | | | 1 | 2" x 29" |
| | | | 1 | 2" x 27" |
| | 6 | 1½" x 42" | 1 | 1½" x 61" |
| | | | 1 | 1½" x 60" |
| | | | 1 | 1½" x 52" |
| | | | 1 | 1½" x 44" |
| **Fabric B** ⅓ yard | 6 | 1½" x 42" | 2 | 1½" x 61" |
| | | | 1 | 1½" x 44" |
| | | | 1 | 1½" x 41" |
| | | | 1 | 1½" x 20" |
| | | | 1 | 1½" x 10" |
| **Fabric C** ⅜ yard | 2 | 3" x 42" | 1 | 3" x 57" |
| | 2 | 2" x 42" | 1 | 2" x 50" |
| | | | 1 | 2" x 30" |
| **Fabric D** ½ yard | 4 | 3" x 42" | 1 | 3" x 63" |
| | | | 1 | 3" x 39" |
| | | | 1 | 3" x 25" |
| **Fabric E** ⅔ yard | 4 | 5½" x 42" | 1 | 5½" x 64" |
| | | | 1 | 5½" x 33" |
| | | | 1 | 5½" x 24" |
| **Fabric F** ⅔ yard | 4 | 3½" x 42" | 1 | 3½" x 58" |
| | | | 1 | 3½" x 49" |
| | | | 1 | 3½" x 14" |
| **First Border** ¼ yard | 6 | 1" x 42" | | |
| **Second Border** ¼ yard | 6 | 1" x 42" | | |
| **Outside Border** ½ yard | 6 | 2½" x 42" | | |
| **Binding** ⅝ yard | 7 | 2¾" x 42" | | |
| Backing - 3 yards Batting - 54" x 71" Removable Fabric Marker | | | | |

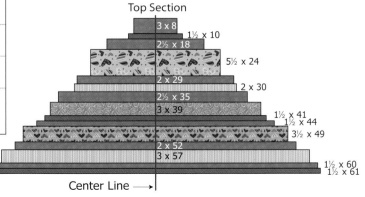

Top Section

3 x 8
1½ x 10
2½ x 18
5½ x 24
2 x 29
2 x 30
2½ x 35
3 x 39
1½ x 41
1½ x 44
3½ x 49
2 x 52
3 x 57
1½ x 60
1½ x 61

Center Line →

Strips of fabric in a variety of widths and patterns are sewn into a soothing, diagonal pattern to create a quietly eye-catching throw. This calm and comforting quilt is perfect to curl up with while reading and relaxing.

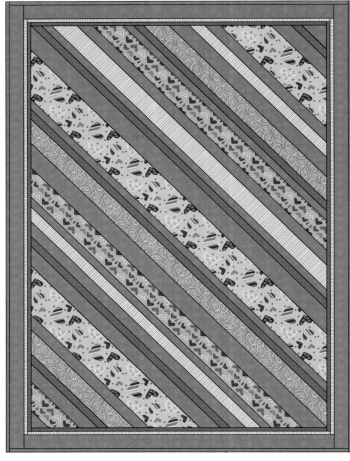

**Delightful Diagonal THROW**
Finished Size: 48" x 65"

5. Align centerlines and refer to diagram below to sew one strip each of the following: 3" x 60", 1½" x 52", 2" x 47", 2½" x 42", 2" x 27", 2½" x 14", and 3" x 8" Fabric A strips; 1½" x 44" and 1½" x 20" Fabric B strips; 2" x 50" Fabric C strip; 3" x 25" Fabric D strip; 5½" x 33" Fabric E strip; and 3½" x 58" and 3½" x 14" Fabric F strips. Press seams in one direction. This completes the Bottom Section.

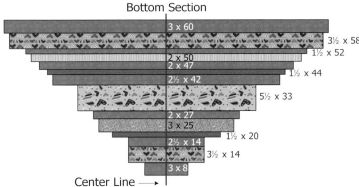

Bottom Section

3 x 60
3½ x 58
1½ x 52
2 x 50
2 x 47
1½ x 44
2½ x 42
5½ x 33
2 x 27
3 x 25
1½ x 20
2½ x 14
3½ x 14
3 x 8

Center Line →

3. Sew one 1½" x 61" Fabric A strip to one 1½" x 61" Fabric B strip matching centerlines. Press.

4. Sew unit from step 3 between one 5½" x 64" Fabric E strip and one 3" x 63" Fabric D strip as shown. Centerlines do not match but are offset by 3". Press. Sew this unit to one 3" x 62" Fabric A strip offsetting center line 4" as shown. Press. This completes the Center Section.

Center Section

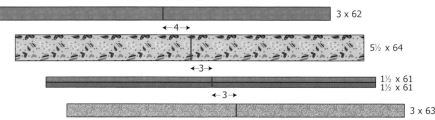

3 x 62
←4→
5½ x 64
←3→
1½ x 61
1½ x 61
←3→
3 x 63

6. Sew Top, Center, and Bottom sections together offsetting the center section centerlines by 1" as shown. Press.

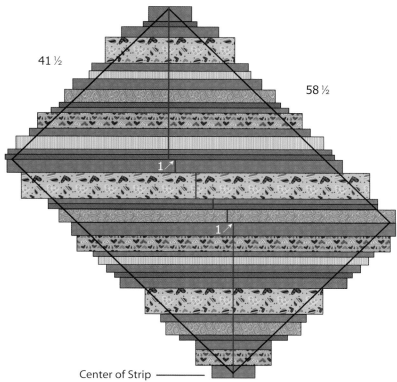

41½

58½

1↗

1↗

Center of Strip ———

## Adding the Borders

1. Using removable fabric marker, draw 41½" x 58½" rectangle on right side of quilt as shown in step 6 diagram placing rectangle at 45-degree angle. Treat this line as the outside of the quilt; First Border edges will line up next to it. This easy method prevents having to sew on the bias edge.

2. Refer to Adding the Borders on page 110. Cut two 1" x 41½" First Border strips. Sew to top and bottom of quilt aligning edges on marked line. Trim top and bottom seams removing excess pieced fabric from underneath. Press seams toward border.

3. Sew 1" x 42" First Border strips together end-to-end to make one continuous 1"-wide First Border strip. Measure quilt through center from top to bottom including borders just added. Cut two 1"-wide First Border strips to this measurement. Sew to sides of quilt. Trim side seams removing excess pieced fabric from underneath. Press.

4. Sew 1"-wide Second Border strips together end-to-end to make one continuous 1"-wide Second Border. Press. Measure quilt through center from side to side. Cut two 1"-wide Second Border strips to this measurement. Sew to top and bottom of quilt. Press seams toward Border.

5. Refer to step 3 to measure, trim, and sew 1"-wide Second Border to sides of quilt. Press.

6. Refer to steps 4 and 5 to join, measure, trim, and sew 2½"-wide Outside Border strips to top, bottom, and sides of quilt. Press.

## Layering and Finishing

1. Cut backing crosswise into two equal pieces. Sew pieces together lengthwise to make one 54" x 80" (approximate) backing piece.

2. Referring to Layering the Quilt on page 110, arrange and baste backing, batting, and top together. Hand or machine quilt as desired.

3. Refer to Binding the Quilt on page 110. Sew 2¾" x 42" binding strips end-to-end to make one continuous 2¾"-wide binding strip. Bind quilt to finish.

# Flowerful Thoughts
# JOURNAL COVER

You record all your thoughts in your journal, so let it say something about you from the outside in by creating a beautiful appliquéd cover for your journal. Not a journalizer? Cover your planner or engagement calendar with a personalized cover.

## Materials Needed

Journal
Cover Fabric
Appliqué Background - Scrap
   One 4½" x 6½"
Flower Appliqués - Scraps
Lightweight Fusible Web - ¼ yard
Iron-on Interfacing
½" Grosgrain Ribbon
Perle Cotton or Embroidery Floss
Beads

## Fabric Requirements and Cutting Instructions

Open journal and lay flat with cover size up. Measure width of journal (back, binding, and front) and add 6¾" - this will be the fabric width measurement. Measure length of journal (top to bottom) and add 1¾" - this will be the fabric length measurement. Ribbon yardage is twice the journal width measurement.

## Adding the Appliqués

Refer to Quick-Fuse Appliqué instructions on page 109. Trace Flower pattern on page 85 on paper side of fusible web. Use appropriate fabrics to prepare all appliqués for fusing.

1. Refer to photo to position and fuse appliqués to 4½" x 6½" Appliqué Background piece. Finish appliqué edges with machine satin stitch or other decorative stitching as desired.

2. Refer to Embroidery Stitch Guide on page 111 for Straight Stitch. Use Perlé cotton or embroidery floss to stitch ¼" from outside edge. Stitch detail to center of flower. Add beads as desired.

3. Fold side edges 2¾" to wrong side of journal cover and press. Wrap cover around journal and position appliqué unit, centering it on front. Remove cover and fuse in place. Finish appliqué unit edges with machine satin stitch or other decorative stitching as desired.

4. Cut interfacing the same size as cover fabric piece. Following manufacturer's instructions fuse interfacing to wrong size of cover.

## Making the Cover

1. Fold each short side (length) ¼" to the wrong side, press and stitch in place.

2. Fold stitched edge 2½" to the right side and press. Using ¼"-wide seam and a basting stitch, sew flap. Repeat for other side. Turn flaps and insert journal to check fit of cover. Adjust flap as needed to make appropriate fit.

3. After flap is adjusted to the correct size, re-stitch using normal stitch-length setting, clip corners, turn, and press. Press top and bottom raw edges of cover to the wrong side matching flap edge.

4. Following manufacturer's instructions, fuse lightweight fusible web to wrong side of ribbon. Cut two lengths of ribbon so each covers raw edge and extends under each flap area a little. Cover raw edges with ribbon and fuse in place.

# Etched Leaves
# WALL ART

Use real leaves and craft paints to create this ephemeral-looking wall art.

## Making the Wall Art

1. Basecoat canvas with Wedgwood Blue paint. Two or more coats of paint may be needed for good coverage. Allow paint to dry thoroughly after each application.

2. Dry brush canvas with small amounts of Slate Blue and Antique White. To dry brush, load a stiff brush with small amount of Slate Blue color. Blot brush on a paper towel removing most of paint. Lightly and rapidly draw brush across canvas to achieve a soft feathery textured effect. Repeat process with Antique White paint, adding just a little texture and movement to the background. Allow to dry. Paint edges of canvas with Spice Brown for contrast.

3. To print leaves onto the prepared canvas, select a leaf and apply paint to back side of leaf as shown. Carefully place leaf, paint side down, on canvas. Tap gently with fingertips to transfer paint and "stick" leaf to canvas.

4. Cover leaf with a paper towel and use a sponge roller or brayer to apply pressure to transfer the paint. Remove paper towel and gently pull leaf straight up, being careful not to smear paint. Apply a few large leaves using Slate Blue as an under layer, then using photo as inspiration, apply leaves in other colors. Allow to dry.

5. Spray canvas with matte spray varnish and allow to dry. To add depth, spread a small amount of antiquing on the canvas and remove most of antiquing with a damp cloth. Keep adding and removing antiquing until desired finish is achieved.

6. Add fine spatters to art piece by mixing Spice Brown paint with water to the consistency of water. Dip bristles of brush into mixed paint then tap brush with finger several times to remove excess paint. Hold brush in one hand, palm down, with index finger on top of metal part of brush and thumb and other fingers loosely wrapped around base of handle. Don't grip brush firmly; allow it to balance against the underside of your wrist. From the wrist, jiggle brush to scatter drops of paint over the surface to be painted. Be sure to practice this technique on a piece of paper before attempting it on your art piece. Remove any excess or too-large spatters with a damp cotton swab. When paint is thoroughly dry, spray again with matte spray varnish and hang as desired.

## Materials Needed

**14" x 18" Stretched Canvas**

**Acrylic Craft Paints** - Delta Ceramcoat® in Wedgwood Blue, Spice Brown, Antique White, and Apple Green; FolkArt® in Slate Blue

**Assorted Paintbrushes & Old Toothbrush**

**Fresh Leaves** - Assorted sizes and shapes. Select leaves with well-defined veins.

**Small Sponge Roller or Brayer**

**FolkArt® Antiquing Medium** - Woodn' Bucket Brown

**Matte Spray Varnish**

Ideas abound in a Creative Corner that's both fun and functional. So corral your supplies and create a space that's as hard working as it is inspirational.

# Creative
# CORNERS

Creative Corners

93

# Creative Energy WALL QUILT

**"X" marks the spot where energy and creativity converge. You'll see something new every time you look at this colorful and compelling quilt, yet sewing is easy and a great way to use scrap strips or honey bun pieces.**

| Creative Energy Wall Quilt Finished Size: 32" x 44" | FIRST CUT | | SECOND CUT | |
|---|---|---|---|---|
| | Number of Strips or Pieces | Dimensions | Number of Pieces | Dimensions |
| Fabric A<br>Blocks Center<br>⅛ yard | 1 | 2½" x 42" | 6* | 2½" squares |
| **Fabric B - Block 1** | | | | |
| Y1<br>⅙ yard | 2 | 1½" x 42" | 4<br>4 | 1½" x 8½"<br>1½" x 2½" |
| Y2<br>⅛ yard | 1 | 1½" x 42" | 4 | 1½" x 4½" |
| Y3<br>⅛ yard | 1 | 1½" x 42" | 4 | 1½" x 6½" |
| Y4<br>⅛ yard | 1 | 1½" x 42" | 4 | 1½" x 8½" |
| Y5<br>⅙ yard | 2 | 1½" x 42" | 4<br>4 | 1½" x 10½"<br>1½" x 4½" |
| Y6<br>⅛ yard | 1 | 1½" x 42" | 4 | 1½" x 2½" |
| Y7<br>⅛ yard | 1 | 1½" x 42" | 4 | 1½" x 6½" |
| Y8<br>⅙ yard | 2 | 1½" x 42" | 4 | 1½" x 10½" |
| **Fabric B - Block 2** | | | | |
| G1<br>⅛ yard | 1 | 1½" x 42" | 4 | 1½" x 2½" |
| G2<br>⅛ yard | 1 | 1½" x 42" | 4 | 1½" x 4½" |
| G3<br>⅛ yard | 1 | 1½" x 42" | 4<br>4 | 1½" x 6½"<br>1½" x 2½" |
| G4<br>⅛ yard | 1 | 1½" x 42" | 4 | 1½" x 8½" |
| G5<br>⅙ yard | 2 | 1½" x 42" | 4 | 1½" x 10½" |
| G6<br>⅛ yard | 1 | 1½" x 42" | 4 | 1½" x 4½" |
| G7<br>⅛ yard | 1 | 1½" x 42" | 4 | 1½" x 6½" |
| G8<br>⅛ yard | 1 | 1½" x 42" | 4 | 1½" x 8½" |
| G9<br>⅙ yard | 2 | 1½" x 42" | 4 | 1½" x 10½" |

| Creative Energy Wall Quilt CONTINUED | FIRST CUT | | SECOND CUT | |
|---|---|---|---|---|
| | Number of Strips or Pieces | Dimensions | Number of Pieces | Dimensions |
| **Fabric B - Block 3** | | | | |
| B1<br>⅙ yard | 2 | 1½" x 42" | 4<br>4 | 1½" x 8½"<br>1½" x 2½" |
| B2<br>⅙ yard | 2 | 1½" x 42" | 4<br>4 | 1½" x 10½"<br>1½" x 4½" |
| B3<br>⅛ yard | 1 | 1½" x 42" | 4 | 1½" x 6½" |
| B4<br>⅙ yard | 2 | 1½" x 42" | 4<br>4 | 1½" x 10½"<br>1½" x 2½" |
| B5<br>⅛ yard | 1 | 1½" x 42" | 4 | 1½" x 4½" |
| B6<br>⅛ yard | 1 | 1½" x 42" | 4 | 1½" x 6½" |
| B7<br>⅛ yard | 1 | 1½" x 42" | 4 | 1½" x 8½" |
| Fabric C<br>Block 1 Accent Squares<br>Assorted Scraps<br>each of 7 Fabrics<br>(Cut from leftover Fabric B Block 3 scraps) | 6* | 1½" squares<br>*cut for each fabric | | |
| Fabric C<br>Block 2 Accent Squares<br>Assorted Scraps<br>each of 8 Fabrics<br>(Cut from leftover Fabric B Block 1 scraps) | 5* | 1½" squares<br>*cut for each fabric | | |
| Fabric C<br>Block 3 Accent Squares<br>Assorted Scraps<br>each of 7 Fabrics<br>(Cut from leftover Outside Border scraps) | 6* | 1½" squares<br>*cut for each fabric | | |
| First Border<br>⅙ yard | 4 | 1" x 42" | 2<br>2 | 1" x 37½"<br>1" x 24½" |
| **Outside Border** | | | | |
| Darks<br>Assorted Fabric A & B Scraps | 36 | 1½" squares | | |
| Lights<br>¼ yard<br>each of 7 Fabrics | 3* | 1½" x 42"<br>*cut for each fabric | 4*<br>11* | 1½" x 20"<br>1½" squares |
| Binding<br>½ yard | 5 | 2¾" x 42" | | |
| Backing - 1½ yards<br>Batting - 38" x 50" | | | | |

## Fabric Requirements and Cutting Instructions

Read all instructions before beginning and use ¼"-wide seam allowances throughout. Read Cutting Strips and Pieces on page 108 prior to cutting fabric.

## Getting Started

This striking wall quilt with its play of color and squares adds stimulation to your workspace. Block measures 12½" square (unfinished). Refer to Accurate Seam Allowance on page 108. Whenever possible use Assembly Line Method on page 108. Press seams in direction of arrows.

## Making Block 1

Use an assortment of different 1½" Fabric C squares to make this block.

1. Sew one 2½" Fabric A square between two 1½" x 2½" Fabric B (Y6) pieces as shown. Press. Make two.

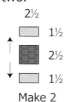

2½
1½
2½
1½

Make 2

2. Sew one 1½" x 2½" Fabric B (Y1) piece between two 1½" Fabric C squares as shown. Press. Make four. Sew unit from step 1 between two of these units as shown. Press. Make two.

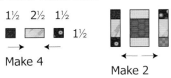

Make 4

Make 2

3. Sew unit from step 2 between two 1½" x 4½" Fabric B (Y5) pieces as shown. Press. Make two.

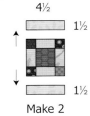

Make 2

4. Sew one 1½" x 4½" Fabric B (Y2) piece between two 1½" Fabric C squares as shown. Press. Make four. Sew unit from step 3 between two of these units as shown. Press. Make two.

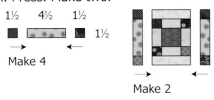

Make 4

Make 2

5. Sew unit from step 4 between two 1½" x 6½" Fabric B (Y7) pieces as shown. Press. Make two.

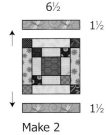

Make 2

6. Sew one 1½" x 6½" Fabric B (Y3) piece between two 1½" Fabric C squares as shown. Press. Make four. Sew unit from step 5 between two of these units as shown. Press. Make two.

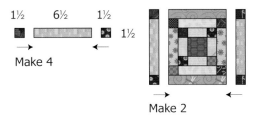

Make 4

Make 2

7. Sew unit from step 6 between two 1½" x 8½" Fabric B (Y1) pieces as shown. Press. Make two.

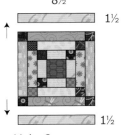

Make 2

8. Sew one 1½" x 8½" Fabric B (Y4) piece between two 1½" Fabric C squares as shown. Press. Make four. Sew unit from step 7 between two of these units as shown. Press. Make two.

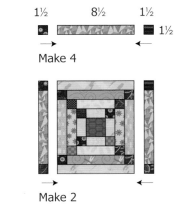

Make 4

Make 2

9. Sew unit from step 8 between two 1½" x 10½" Fabric B (Y8) pieces as shown. Press. Make two.

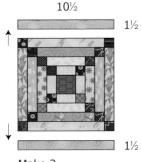

Make 2

## Creative Energy WALL QUILT
Finished Size: 32" x 44"

10. Sew one 1½" x 10½" Fabric B (Y5) piece between two 1½" Fabric C squares as shown. Press. Make four. Sew unit from step 9 between two of these units as shown. Press. Make two and label Block 1. Block measures 12½" square.

**Block 1**

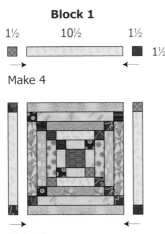

Make 2
Block measures 12½" square

## Making Block 2 and Block 3

Diagrams below are labeled with Fabric B placements. Refer to cutting chart to use an assortment of different colored Fabric C squares to make these blocks. Refer to Block 1 instructions steps 1-10 to make two each of Block 2 and Block 3. Block measures 12½" square.

**Block 2**

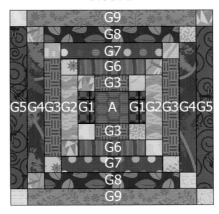

Make 2
Block measures 12½" square

**Block 3**

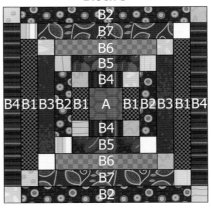

Make 2
Block measures 12½" square

## Assembling the Quilt

1. Referring to photo on page 95 and layout, sew one Block 1 and one Block 2 together. Press. Sew one Block 3 and one Block 1 together. Press. Sew one Block 2 and one Block 3 together. Press.

2. Refer to photo on page 95 and layout, to sew rows from step 1 together. Press.

## Adding the Borders

1. Sew 1" x 24½"-wide First Border strips to top and bottom of quilt. Press seams toward border.

2. Sew two 1" x 37½"-wide First Border strips to sides of quilt. Press.

3. Sew together lengthwise three 1½" x 20" Outside Border fabric strips to make a strip set. Press. Make eight using different fabric combinations. Cut strip sets into one hundred 1½"-wide assorted segments as shown.

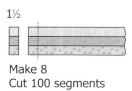

1½

Make 8
Cut 100 segments

4. Sew three units from step 3 together as shown. Press. Make eight in assorted fabric combinations.

Make 8
(in assorted fabric combinations)

5. Cut remaining Outside Border strips into 1½" squares for the following step. Sew together two 1½" Outside Border Light squares and one 1½" Outside Border Dark square to make a set. Press. Make thirty-six 1½"-wide segments as shown varying the placement of Fabric C Accent squares.

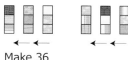

Make 36
(in assorted fabric combinations)

6. Arrange two units from step 3 and one unit from step 5 together as shown. Press. Make thirty-six in assorted fabric combinations.

Make 36
(in assorted fabric combinations)

7. Referring to photo on page 95 and layout on page 97, arrange and sew together one unit from step 3, and eight units from steps 4 and 6. Make two. Press. Sew to top and bottom of quilt. Press.

8. Referring to photo on page 95 and layout on page 97, arrange and sew together one unit from step 3 and fourteen units from steps 4 and 6. Make two. Sew to sides of quilt. Press.

## Layering and Finishing

1. Referring to Layering the Quilt on page 110, arrange and baste backing, batting, and top together. Hand or machine quilt as desired.

2. Refer to Binding the Quilt on page 110. Sew 2¾" x 42" binding strips end-to-end to make one continuous 2¾"-wide binding strip. Bind quilt to finish.

It's in the details

Round up your ribbon and bottle up your buttons in repurposed jars. When the food is gone, use clean wide-mouth jars to hold small supplies. Paint the lids to match your décor.

A wire garden shelf finds new life when repurposed to hold craft supplies. Paints, brushes, trims, buttons and beads are easy to see and tape and scissors are easy to find on the handy hooks.

# Pretty Posy
# PIN CUSHION

Make this cute pin cushion in an evening and enjoy its fanciful design and beautiful color every time you're in your Creative Corner.

## Materials Needed

Pin Cushion Top & Bottom - Wool scraps
    Two 6" squares

Gusset - Wool scrap
    One 2¾" x 13"

Appliqué - Assorted wool scraps

Lightweight Fusible Web - ⅙ yard

Embroidery Floss

Polyester Fiberfill

Bean Bag Pellets

Removable Fabric Marker

## Getting Started

An adorable wool pincushion is a great gift to give to your quilting friends.

## Adding the Appliqués

Refer to appliqué instructions on page 109. Our instructions are for Quick-Fuse Appliqué, but if you prefer hand appliqué, add ¼"-wide seam allowances for cotton fabrics.

1. Refer to Circle Templates on page 111. Trace 5" circle on template plastic or pattern paper. Cut out circle on drawn line. Trace 5" circle template on one 6" Pin Cushion square.

2. Use patterns to trace small flower and three leaves on paper side of fusible web. Use appropriate fabrics to prepare all appliqués for fusing.

3. Refer to photo to position and fuse appliqués to marked square from step 1 centering design in circle. Finish appliqué edges with machine blanket stitch or use two strands of embroidery floss to stitch by hand or a combination of techniques.

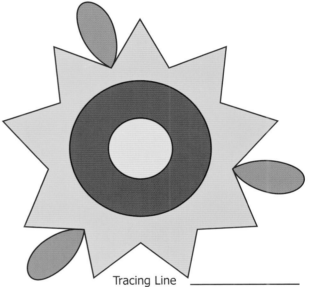

Tracing Line _____

## Making the Pin Cushion

1. Check appliquéd 5" circle for possible shrinkage due to finishing appliqué edges. Redraw 5" circle if needed. Cut out circle on drawn line. Cut 5" circle from bottom fabric piece.

2. Using a ¼"-wide seam, sew 2¾" x 13" Gusset piece short sides together to form a loop. Press. Using a ½"-wide seam, sew appliqué circle to gusset.

3. Using a ½"-wide seam, sew bottom circle to unit from step 2 leaving a 3" opening for turning.

4. Fill pincushion with polyester fiberfill then add beanbag pellets to bottom area to add weight to piece. Hand stitch opening closed.

5. Refer to photo and Embroidery Stitches on page 111 for Straight Stitch. Using six strands of embroidery floss, hand-stitch along circle and gusset edges as shown.

# Create
# WALL ART

## Materials Needed

Background - ¼ yard (each of 6 fabrics)
   Six 9" x 11"

Six 5" x 7" Canvas Frames
   OR Twelve 7" Stretcher Bars
   Twelve 5" Stretcher Bars
   Backing & Batting - Six 9" x 11"

Lightweight Fusible Web - ⅔ yard

Rickrack - ¼ yard (Optional)

Assorted Buttons

Embroidery Floss

Staple Gun & Staples

Tacky Glue

Picture or Sawtooth Hangers

## Getting Started

Make an inspirational statement with these wall art pieces.

## Adding the Appliqués

Refer to appliqué instructions on page 109. Our instructions are for Quick-Fuse Appliqué.

1. Refer to Word Art tip box for letter template information. Trace letters on paper side of fusible web. Use appropriate fabrics to prepare all appliqués for fusing.

2. Refer to photo on page 101 to position and fuse appliqués to 9" x 11" Background piece. Finish appliqué edges with machine satin stitch or other decorative stitching as desired.

3. Add embellishments as desired now or after framing is completed.

## Making the Wall Art

1. If using interlocking stretcher bars slide two 5" and two 7" bars together. Check for square by measuring from corner to corner. Staple at corners. Note: if using canvas frames omit step 2, batting and backing fabric. Center wrong side of appliqué unit on canvas frame.

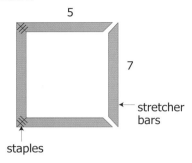

2. Layer appliqué unit (wrong side facing up) batting, and backing (right side facing up). Center frame on top of unit.

3. Pull fabric around frame, staple in the middle on each side pulling fabric tightly to obtain good tension. Turn piece over to check letter placement and adjust as needed. Continue process, working from center, stretching and stapling fabric, stopping at corners.

Back View

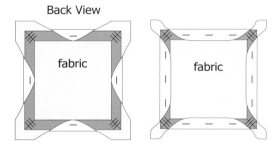

4. Pull corner tight and check front to make sure fabric is taut. Fold excess fabric at 90°, crease, and form corner. Staple tightly to back.

5. Attach a wire picture hanger or sawtooth hanger to back of each wall piece. Add any additional embellishments as desired.

Take one inspirational word, mix it with fun fabrics, add exuberant embellishments, and you have wall art that says it all.

## Word Art - Appliqués
Use your computer to create a pattern for the inspirational word that you select. We used a standard Microsoft Office Word font, Franklin Gothic Bold in 600 pt, but you can use any font that is broad and easy to read and fits the 5" x 7" format. If using Quick Fuse Appliqué method, reverse letters (mirror image) and trace on paper side of fusible web.

## Word Art - Scrapbook
If you prefer, use scrapbook supplies instead of fabric to make your word art. Just paint the sides of each canvas to match the paper you select. Use stickers, rub-ons, and other scrapbook embellishments for decoration.

# Sew Happy TOTE

Organize all your sewing essentials in this tote that can easily go from home to class or quilting bee. A wooden garden tote is repurposed for this handy carry-all. Use our sewing artwork to decorate your tote.

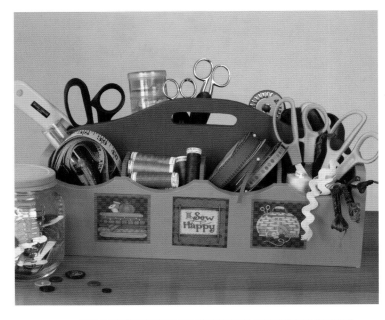

1. Sand tote to prepare it for painting. Remove sanding residue with a soft damp cloth.

2. Paint center divider/handle Spice Brown. Several coats of paint may be needed for good coverage. Allow paint to dry thoroughly after each coat of paint.

3. Paint dividers and sides with Burnt Orange paint. Several coats of paint may be needed for good coverage.

4. Paint outside and rim with Hauser Light Green Paint. Several coats of paint may be needed for good coverage.

5. When paint is thoroughly dry, spray tote with varnish.

6. Copy Sewing Artwork (page 103) using a color copier. Carefully cut each square from copy paper using a ruler and craft knife. Using paintbrush, apply Mod Podge to back of one artwork square, position on tote where desired, and carefully smooth out air bubbles. Repeat for each artwork square. Apply another coat of Mod Podge over each artwork square and front of tote to seal.

## Materials Needed

- Wood Tote
- Sandpaper
- Acrylic Craft Paints – Delta Ceramcoat® Spice Brown; Americana® Hauser Light Green and Burnt Orange
- Satin Spray Varnish
- Mod Podge® Satin
- Assorted Paintbrushes
- Ruler and Craft Knife
- Gesso
- Color Copies of Sewing Artwork page 103 (Optional)

**Photo boxes** (approx. 7½" x 11" x 4¼") come in many colors and are readily available at craft stores. Look for solid color boxes that will coordinate with your fabrics. Covering the lids only is fast and efficient. Cut a piece of fabric large enough to cover your lid and wrap around to the inside (approx. 14" x 17"). Fuse heavyweight fusible web to the back of fabric and adhere fabric to lid with an iron, cutting and trimming fabric as needed at corners. Or, coat the lid with decoupage medium and adhere fabric, stretching and rubbing with fingers to eliminate air bubbles. Trim fabric at corners as needed. Decorate lid with ribbon, buttons, and other embellishments as desired.

# Inspiration Station
# STORAGE

Storage solutions can be beautiful as well as functional. Dress up magazine holders and photo storage boxes with fabric for stylish and creative containers. If desired, use our sewing artwork to embellish the containers.

Inexpensive cardboard **magazine holders** (approx. 9½" x 12½" x 4") are available at Ikea and other stores. We found that decoupage works best to cover the magazine holders. Start with a rectangle of fabric approximately 15" x 30". Spread decoupage on one side and back of cardboard holder, lay holder on fabric then wrap and smooth fabric onto those two sides. Add decoupage to other sides and continue wrapping and smoothing fabric. Cut fabric where needed for a smooth fit, making sure that you have at least an inch on all sides to wrap to the inside of the magazine holder and to wrap to the bottom. If holder has a metal identification label, roughly cut over the label, but leave the fine trimming for after the decoupage has dried. It will be a lot easier to cut with a craft knife when the fabric is dry and stiffened with decoupage. If desired, embellish the covered holder with ribbon, buttons, or use decoupage to adhere sewing artwork.

*Permission to photocopy page 103 is granted by Debbie Mumm Inc. to successfully complete the Sew Happy Tote.*

# Sit 'n Sew
## CHAIR CUSHION

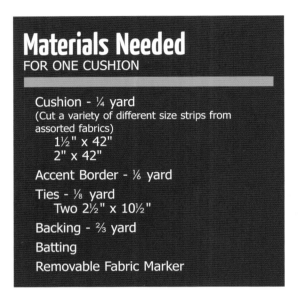

### Materials Needed
#### FOR ONE CUSHION

Cushion - ¼ yard
(Cut a variety of different size strips from assorted fabrics)
    1½" x 42"
    2" x 42"

Accent Border - ⅙ yard

Ties - ⅛ yard
    Two 2½" x 10½"

Backing - ⅔ yard

Batting

Removable Fabric Marker

## Getting Started

Quilt as you go method was used for this chair cushion. We added additional batting to cushion to give it some added loft without adding to the depth of the cushion. We recommend using a walking foot for this project.

## Making the Chair Cushion

1. Measure seat width and length. Divide seat into four sections. Note: These might be rectangular. Cut backing and batting pieces 4" larger than Quarter Section measurements. Cut four.

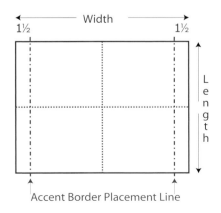

2. Layer backing and batting pieces together then place two strips right sides together along one corner aligning fabric with ruler's 45° angle as shown.

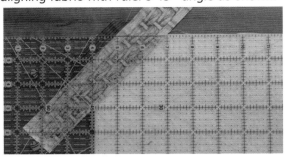

3. Using ¼"-wide seam, stitch fabric to batting unit as shown. Note: To determine strip length, place strip right side up next to previous strip and trim strip close to batting edge.

¼"-wide seam             Press.

4. Continue adding strips to unit following same procedure until batting and backing area is covered. Make four. Note: Watch angle of strip placement for quarter sections.

5. Refer to photo to arrange units from step 4. Square inside (center) corners only of units and trim. Leave excess on sides untrimmed.

6. Refer to photo to arrange units from step 5 noting angle directions. Sew units together using ¼"-wide seam. Refer to Twisting Seams on page 110. Press.

7. Using removable fabric marker, mark unit from step 6 to original seat measurement centering intersection of seams. Measure and mark 1½" inside edge of width as shown in step 1 diagram.

**A decorative chair cushion will make it easy for you to sit and sew and enjoy your Creative Corner. A quilt-as-you-go method makes this cushion fast and easy to make. Don't need a chair cushion? Use this pattern to make pillows or placemats.**

8. Cut two Accent Border 1½" x chair length measurement. Align border strip on marked line (step 7).

9. Using ¼"-wide seam, sew border to pieced unit. Press. Repeat steps 7-8 for other side. Cut unit ½" larger than original seat measurement and sides even with Accent Border outside edge.

10. Cut a piece of backing fabric the same size as unit from step 9. Place pieces right sides together. Using ¼"-wide seam, stitch around all edges, leaving a 10" opening on one side for turning. Clip corners, turn, and press.

11. Cut six batting pieces the size of cushion, layer and baste them together. Trim if needed. Insert into cushion and hand-stitch opening closed.

12. This chair cushion is tied at the center back. Tie quantity may vary depending on chair style. Press short ends of 2½" x 10½" Tie piece ¼" to the wrong side. Fold tie in half lengthwise and press. Open and fold raw edges to center pressed line. Press. Fold again in half lengthwise. Press. Top stitch folds in place. Make two.

13. Sew ties to chair cushion as desired.

# Embellished BASKET LINER

## Materials Needed

Basket (with handles)

Basket Fabric - ½ - ¾ yard
(Quantity will vary depending on basket size)
    Four 2½" x 10½" (Ties)

Trim - 2 yards or basket perimeter

Assorted Buttons & Beads

## Fabric Requirements and Cutting Instructions

Read all instructions before beginning and use ¼"-wide seam allowances throughout. Use chart to calculate and cut fabric pieces to fit purchased basket.

1. Measure basket width, length, and depth as shown. Add ½" to length and width measurements for seam allowance. Cut one piece of fabric using width, depth and length measurements.

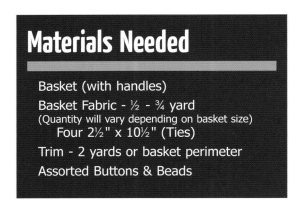

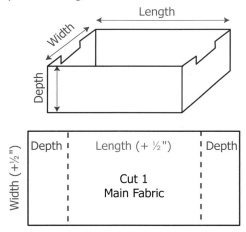

2. Add ½" to length and depth measurements for seam allowance. Cut two pieces of fabric using these measurements.

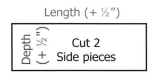

3. Measure the basket from one basket handle to the next as shown. Add 3" to this measurement. Cut two pieces 4" x this measurements for flaps. Note: If a wider flap is desired change the 4" measurement accordingly.

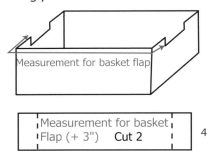

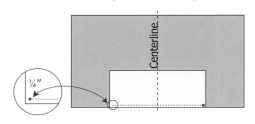

## Making the Basket Liner

1. Mark centerlines on Main Fabric and Side pieces. Mark side pieces ¼" from each corner. This will be your stitching starting and stopping points.

2. Place one marked Side panel on Main Fabric right sides together matching centerlines. Using ¼"-wide seam, stitch starting and stopping at ¼" marks.

Start stitching at ¼" mark

3. Pivot fabric and align main fabric corner to side piece top corner as shown. Start stitching at mark and stitch to corner.

Pivot fabric at ¼" mark

Baskets are great when it comes to organizing, but wicker can snag fabric and yarn. These basket liners are a pretty way to add color, charm, and functionality to your baskets.

4. Pivot fabric and align other corners as shown below. Starting at the top, stitch down to ¼" mark. Repeat steps 4-6 to stitch to other side.

Lining Inside Unit

5. To make a narrow hem turn flap short side under ¼" to the wrong side press. Fold under another ¼" and press. Topstitch. Repeat for other side. Make two.

6. For one long side of flap, fold under ¼" to the wrong side. Press. Fold under another ¼" and press. Topstitch. Refer to photo to add trim and embellishments to lower section of flap as desired. Make two.

7. Place one Flap piece right sides together with main unit aligning centerlines. When pinning Flap to unit take a ½" tuck at each corner's seamline. Sew flap to unit. Press. Repeat for other side.

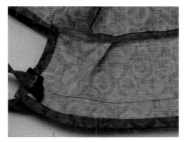

8. Fold under raw edge of main fabric handle area matching flap seam line. Stitch in place.

9. Press short ends of 2½" x 10½" Tie piece ¼" to the wrong side. Fold tie in half lengthwise and press. Open and fold raw edges to center pressed line. Press. Fold again in half lengthwise. Press. Top stitch folds in place. Make four.

10. Sew ties to inside of flap on each side of handle.

# General Directions

## Cutting Strips and Pieces

We recommend washing cotton fabrics in cold water and pressing before making projects in this book. Using a rotary cutter, see-through ruler, and a cutting mat, cut the strips and pieces for the project. If indicated on the Cutting Chart, some will need to be cut again into smaller strips and pieces. Make second cuts in order shown to maximize use of fabric. The yardage amounts are based on an approximate fabric width of 42" and Fat Quarters are based on 18" x 22" pieces.

## Pressing

Pressing is very important for accurate seam allowances. Press seams using either steam or dry heat with an "up and down" motion. Do not use side-to-side motion as this will distort the unit or block. Set the seam by pressing along the line of stitching, then press seams to one side as indicated by project instructions and diagram arrows.

## Twisting Seams

When a block has several seams meeting in the center as shown, there will be less bulk if seam allowances are pressed in a circular type direction and the center intersection "twisted". Remove 1-2 stitches in the seam allowance to enable the center to twist and lay flat. This technique aids in quilt assembly by allowing the seams to fall opposite each other when repeated blocks are next to each other. The technique works well with 4-patch blocks, pinwheel blocks, and quarter-square triangle blocks.

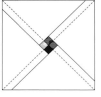

## Accurate Seam Allowance

Accurate seam allowances are always important, but especially when the blocks contain many pieces and the quilt top contains multiple pieced borders. If each seam is off as little as ⅟₁₆", you'll soon find yourself struggling with components that just won't fit.

To ensure seams are a perfect ¼"-wide, try this simple test: Cut three strips of fabric, each exactly 1½" x 12". With right sides together, and long raw edges aligned, sew two strips together, carefully maintaining a ¼" seam. Press seam to one side. Add the third strip to complete the strip set. Press and measure. The finished strip set should measure 3½" x 12". The center strip should measure 1"-wide, the two outside strips 1¼"-wide, and the seam allowances exactly ¼".

If your measurements differ, check to make sure that seams have been pressed flat. If strip set still doesn't "measure up," try stitching a new strip set, adjusting the seam allowance until a perfect ¼"-wide seam is achieved.

## Assembly Line Method

Whenever possible, use an assembly line method. Position pieces right sides together and line up next to sewing machine. Stitch first unit together, then continue sewing others without breaking threads. When all units are sewn, clip threads to separate. Press seams in direction of arrows as shown in step-by-step project diagrams.

## Quick Corner Triangles

Quick corner triangles are formed by simply sewing fabric squares to other squares or rectangles. The directions and diagrams with each project illustrate what size pieces to use and where to place squares on the corresponding piece. Follow steps 1–3 below to make quick corner triangle units.

1. With pencil and ruler, draw diagonal line on wrong side of fabric square that will form the triangle. This will be your sewing line.

   Sewing line

2. With right sides together, place square on corresponding piece. Matching raw edges, pin in place, and sew ON drawn line. Trim off excess fabric, leaving ¼"-wide seam allowance as shown.

   Trim ¼" away from sewing line

3. Press seam in direction of arrow as shown in step-by-step project diagram. Measure completed quick corner triangle unit to ensure the greatest accuracy.

   Finished quick corner triangle unit

## Fussy Cut

To make a "fussy cut," carefully position ruler or template over a selected design in fabric. Include seam allowances before cutting desired pieces.

# Quick-Fuse Appliqué

Quick-fuse appliqué is a method of adhering appliqué pieces to a background with fusible web. For quick and easy results, simply quick-fuse appliqué pieces in place. Use sewable, lightweight fusible web for the projects in this book unless otherwise indicated. Finish raw edges with stitching as desired. Laundering is not recommended unless edges are finished.

1. With paper side up, lay fusible web over appliqué pattern. Leaving ½" space between pieces, trace all elements of design. Cut around traced pieces, approximately ¼" outside traced line.

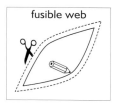

2. With paper side up, position and press fusible web to wrong side of selected fabrics. Follow manufacturer's directions for iron temperature and fusing time. Cut out each piece on traced line.

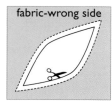

3. Remove paper backing from pieces. A thin film will remain on wrong side of fabric. Position and fuse all pieces of one appliqué design at a time onto background, referring to photos for placement. Fused design will be the reverse of traced pattern.

# Appliqué Pressing Sheet

An appliqué pressing sheet is very helpful when there are many small elements to apply using a quick-fuse appliqué technique. The pressing sheet allows small items to be bonded together before applying them to the background. The sheet is coated with a special material that prevents fusible web from adhering permanently to the sheet. Follow manufacturer's directions. Remember to let fabric cool completely before lifting it from the appliqué sheet. If not cooled, the fusible web could remain on the sheet instead of on the fabric.

For accurate layout, place a line drawing of finished project under pressing sheet. Use this as a guide to adhere pieces.

# Machine Appliqué

This technique should be used when you are planning to launder quick-fuse projects. Several different stitches can be used: small narrow zigzag stitch, satin stitch, blanket stitch, or another decorative machine stitch. Use an open toe appliqué foot if your machine has one. Use a stabilizer to obtain even stitches and help prevent puckering. Always practice first to check machine settings.

1. Fuse all pieces following Quick-Fuse Appliqué directions.

2. Cut a piece of stabilizer large enough to extend beyond the area to be stitched. Pin to the wrong side of fabric.

3. Select thread to match appliqué.

4. Following the order that appliqués were positioned, stitch along the edges of each section. Anchor beginning and ending stitches by tying off or stitching in place two or three times.

5. Complete all stitching, then remove stabilizer.

# Hand Appliqué

Hand appliqué is easy when you start out with the right supplies. Cotton and machine embroidery thread are easy to work with. Pick a color that matches the appliqué fabric as closely as possible. Use appliqué or silk pins for holding shapes in place and a long, thin needle, such as a sharp, for stitching.

1. Make a template for every shape in the appliqué design. Use a dotted line to show where pieces overlap.

2. Place template on right side of appliqué fabric. Trace around template.

3. Cut out shapes ¼" beyond traced line.

4. Position shapes on background fabric, referring to quilt layout. Pin shapes in place.

5. When layering and stitching appliqué shapes, always work from background to foreground. Where shapes overlap, do not turn under and stitch edges of bottom pieces. Turn and stitch the edges of the piece on top.

6. Use the traced line as your turn-under guide. Entering from the wrong side of the appliqué shape, bring the needle up on the traced line. Using the tip of the needle, turn under the fabric along the traced line. Using blind stitch, stitch along folded edge to join the appliqué shape to the background fabric. Turn under and stitch about ¼" at a time.

## Adding the Borders

1. Measure quilt through the center from side to side. Trim two border strips to this measurement. Sew to top and bottom of quilt. Press seams toward border.

2. Measure quilt through the center from top to bottom, including borders added in step 1. Trim border strips to this measurement. Sew to sides and press. Repeat to add additional borders.

## Layering the Quilt

1. Cut backing and batting 4" to 8" larger than quilt top.

2. Lay pressed backing on bottom (right side down), batting in middle, and pressed quilt top (right side up) on top. Make sure everything is centered and that backing and batting are flat. Backing and batting will extend beyond quilt top.

3. Begin basting in center and work toward outside edges. Baste vertically and horizontally, forming a 3"–4" grid. Baste or pin completely around edge of quilt top. Quilt as desired. Remove basting.

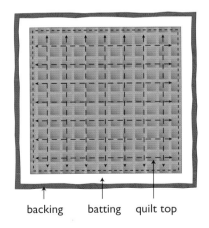

backing    batting    quilt top

## Binding the Quilt

1. Trim batting and backing to ¼" beyond raw edge of quilt top. This will add fullness to binding.

2. Join binding strips to make one continuous strip if needed. To join, place strips perpendicular to each other, right sides together, and draw a diagonal line. Sew on drawn line and trim triangle extensions, leaving a ¼"-wide seam allowance. Continue stitching ends together to make the desired length. Press seams open.

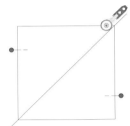

←trim

3. Fold and press binding strips in half lengthwise with wrong sides together.

4. Measure quilt through center from side to side. Cut two binding strips to this measurement. Lay binding strips on top and bottom edges of quilt top with raw edges of binding and quilt top aligned. Sew through all layers, ¼" from quilt edge. Press binding away from quilt top.

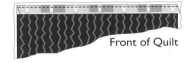

Front of Quilt

5. Measure quilt through center from top to bottom, including binding just added. Cut two binding strips to this measurement and sew to sides through all layers, including binding just added. Press.

6. Folding top and bottom first, fold binding around to back then repeat with sides. Press and pin in position. Hand-stitch binding in place using a blind stitch.

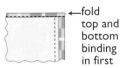

←fold top and bottom binding in first

## Making Bias Strips

1. Refer to Fabric Requirements and Cutting Instructions for the amount of fabric required for the specific bias needed.

2. Remove selvages from the fabric piece and cut into a square. Mark edge with straight pin where selvages were removed as shown. Cut square once diagonally into two equal 45° triangles. (For larger squares, fold square in half diagonally and gently press fold. Open fabric square and cut on fold.)

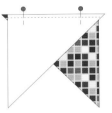

3. Place pinned edges right sides together and stitch along edge with a ¼" seam. Press seam open.

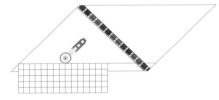

4. Using a ruler and rotary cutter, cut bias strips to width specified in quilt directions.

5. Each strip has a diagonal end. To join, place strips perpendicular to each other, right sides together, matching diagonal cut edges and allowing tips of angles to extend approximately ¼" beyond edges. Sew ¼"-wide seams. Continue stitching ends together to make the desired length. Press seams open. Cut strips into recommended lengths according to quilt directions.

# Finishing Pillows

1. Layer batting between pillow top and lining. Baste. Hand or machine quilt as desired. Trim batting and lining even with raw edge of pillow top.

2. Narrow hem one long edge of each backing piece by folding under ¼" to wrong side. Press. Fold under ¼" again to wrong side. Press. Stitch along folded edge.

3. With sides up, lay one backing piece over second piece so hemmed edges overlap, making backing unit the same measurement as the pillow top. Baste backing pieces together at top and bottom where they overlap.

4. With right sides together, position and pin pillow top to backing. Using ¼"-wide seam, sew around edges, trim corners, turn right side out, and press.

## Pillow Forms

Cut two pieces of fabric to size specified in project's materials needed list. Place right sides together, aligning raw edges. Using ¼"-wide seam, sew around all edges, leaving 5" opening for turning. Trim corners and turn right side out. Stuff to desired fullness with polyester fiberfill and hand-stitch opening closed.

## Tips for Felting Wool

1. Wet wool fabric or WoolFelt™ with hot water. Do not mix colors as dyes may run.

2. Blot wool with a dry towel and place both towel and wool in dryer on high heat until thoroughly dry. The result is a thicker, fuller fabric that will give added texture to the wool. Pressing felted wool is not recommended, as it will flatten the texture. Most wools will shrink 15-30% when felted, adjust yardage accordingly.

## Embroidery Stitch Guide

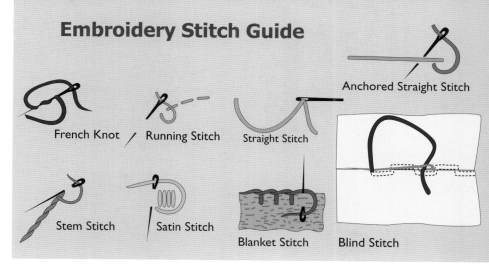

French Knot / Running Stitch / Straight Stitch / Anchored Straight Stitch

Stem Stitch / Satin Stitch / Blanket Stitch / Blind Stitch

## Circle Templates

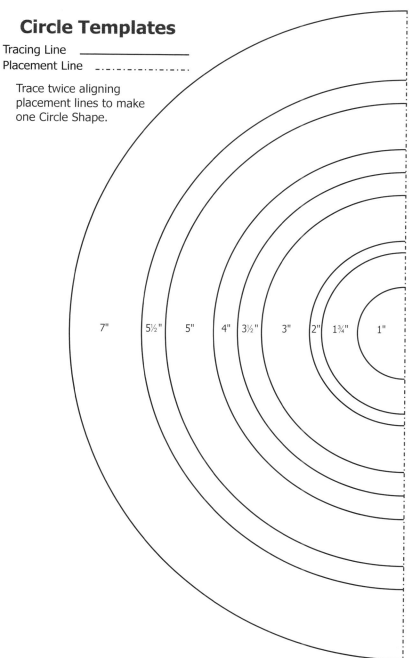

Tracing Line _____

Placement Line _ · _ · _ · _ · _

Trace twice aligning placement lines to make one Circle Shape.

7" 5½" 5" 4" 3½" 3" 2" 1¾" 1"

## About Debbie Mumm

A talented designer, author, and entrepreneur, Debbie Mumm has been creating charming artwork and quilt designs for more than twenty years.

Debbie got her start in the quilting industry in 1986 with her unique and simple-to-construct quilt patterns. Since that time, she has authored more than fifty books featuring quilting and home decorating projects and has led her business to become a multi-faceted enterprise that includes publishing, fabric design, and licensed art divisions.

Known world-wide for the many licensed products that feature her designs, Debbie loves to bring traditional elements together with fresh palettes and modern themes to create the look of today's country.

## Designs by Debbie Mumm

Special thanks to my creative teams:

### Editorial & Project Design

Carolyn Ogden: Publications & Marketing Manager
Nancy Kirkland: Quilt Designer/Seamstress
Georgie Gerl: Technical Writer/Editor
Carolyn Lowe: Technical Editor
Anita Pederson: Machine Quilter

### Book Design & Production

Monica Ziegler: Graphic Designer • Tom Harlow: Graphics Manager
Lori Scott: Administrative Assistant

### Photography

Tom Harlow, Debbie Mumm® Graphics Studio
Carolyn Ogden: Photo Stylist

### Art Team

Kathy Arbuckle: Artist/Designer • Gil-Jin Foster: Artist
Jackie Saling: Designer

Special thanks to Nick and Carolyn Ogden for opening their home for indoor photography. Thanks to Jackie Saling and Bill Sims for welcoming us to their beautiful garden for outdoor photography.

The Debbie Mumm® Sewing Studio exclusively uses Bernina® sewing machines.

## Discover More from Debbie Mumm®

*Debbie Mumm's®
I Care with Quilts*

96-page, soft cover

*Debbie Mumm's®
HomeComings*

96-page, soft cover

*Debbie Mumm's®
Cuddle Quilts for
Little Girls and Boys*

96-page, soft cover

*Debbie Mumm's®
Colors from Nature*

96-page, soft cover

©2010 Debbie Mumm

All rights reserved. This publication is protected under federal copyright laws. Reproduction or distribution of this publication or any other Leisure Arts publication, including publications which are out of print, is prohibited unless specifically authorized. This includes, but is not limited to, any form of reproduction or distribution on or through the Internet, including posting, scanning, or e-mail transmission.

The information in this publication is presented in good faith, but no warranty is given, nor results guaranteed. Since we have no control over physical conditions surrounding the application of information herein contained, Leisure Arts, Inc. and Debbie Mumm, Inc. disclaim any liability for untoward results.

Library of Congress Control Number: 2009943936

### Produced by:

Debbie Mumm, Inc.
1116 E. Westview Court
Spokane, WA 99218
(509) 466-3572
Fax (509) 466-6919

www.debbiemumm.com

### Published by:

Leisure Arts, Inc
5701 Ranch Drive
Little Rock, AR • 72223
www.leisurearts.com

Available at local fabric and craft shops or at **debbiemumm.com**